VIEWING
GLOUCESTERSHIRE

VIEWING GLOUCESTERSHIRE

Gloucestershire through the Eyes of its Authors

Alan Pilbeam

NONSUCH

First published 2006

Nonsuch Publishing Limited
The Mill, Brimscombe Port, Stroud, Gloucestershire, GL5 2QG
www.nonsuch-publishing.com

Nonsuch Publishing is an imprint of Tempus Publishing Group

British Library Cataloguing in Publication Data.
A catalogue record for this book is available from the British Library.

ISBN 1-84588-063-3
ISBN-13 (from January 2007) 978-1-84588-063-7

Typesetting and origination by Nonsuch Publishing Limited
Printed in Great Britain by Oaklands Book Services Limited

CONTENTS

INTRODUCTION

No two people see exactly the same things as they view a landscape together. This is not primarily as a result of variations in eye sight. Our brains cannot cope with all the visual stimuli available to us, so we inevitably select what we see. Items that stand out from their surroundings by their size, movement, newness, or contrasting colours are commonly noticed, but beyond these we see what we look for. The latter is influenced by our knowledge, interests and experience and so varies from person to person. So a farmer, an architect, an estate agent and a geologist will see different things as together they look at the same view and the only way we can be really sure of what another person sees is by what they describe to us.

In this small book we look at the descriptions of Gloucestershire landscapes given by fifteen different observers, extracting from their writings the details that made most impression on them.

The earliest is William Gilpin, who in 1770 travelled by boat down the Wye from Ross to Chepstow looking for picturesque views. He not only describes the views he discovered along this border of the county but explains why they were picturesque and thereby has influenced the perceptions of tourists to the Wye valley and elsewhere ever since. His book was seminal.

We follow Gilpin with John Keble, whose collection of poems in the *Christian Year* was read by most educated people in England in the early nineteenth century. Keble draws some of his inspiration from the gentle landscapes around Fairford, seeing here in the natural world signs of the spiritual.

Spanning several decades of the first half of the nineteenth century are the diaries of Francis Witts. He was the Rector of Upper Slaughter, a magistrate and well-to-do. He travelled widely in the county, both for social reasons and in the course of duty. His diaries describe the changes he noticed, especially in transport and industry and in the urban growth of Cheltenham.

At about the same time H.G. Nicholls, Vicar of Drybrook, was researching the history of the Forest of Dean, perusing old notebooks and the minutes of the Miners' Court. He gives us the first written account of the industry of the Forest and an insight into the lives of his parishioners.

The scenery and rural economy of the Cotswolds at the end of the nineteenth century is lovingly described by J. Arthur Gibbs. His book *A Cotswold Village* was centred on Bibury. It was the first to draw tourists to the Cotswolds and the knowledge he acquired of country sports was the chief source of information for later writers, including H.A. Evans.

Evans made a cycle tour of the north and central Cotswolds at the beginning of the twentieth century and subsequently wrote a tourists' guide for Macmillan's *Highways and Byways* series. The guide is still useful for today's tourist and it is distinguished by the fine engravings of F.L. Griggs.

One of the visitors to the Cotswolds who followed this guide was Norman Jewson and many years later he reminisced on that early visit which changed the whole course of his life. He was introduced to the Arts and Crafts movement flourishing at Sapperton and committed his life to the continuity of traditional Cotswold architecture. He also had a unique insight into the furniture making and building work of Gimson and the Barnsleys.

The First World War checked the progress of the Arts and Crafts movement and also took away from Gloucestershire its two most famous poets. Ivor Gurney and Will Harvey were friends from their youth and express in their poems their love of their county. Some of their most evocative work came from the trenches of France and the prisoner of war camps in Germany, as they recalled what they had left behind.

Memories of a friendship with an old villager at Saintbury provided Algernon Gissing with the stimulus to retrace his steps, originally made at the end of the nineteenth century in the north Cotswolds. He again walked the old footpaths, experiencing afresh the joys of the countryside. His descriptions are so clear one can follow from an Ordnance Survey map the routes he took.

Our next three writers were each brought up in Gloucestershire and vividly recall their childhood experiences as they freely explored their home neighbourhoods. For their feel for the place and the quality of their prose they are outstanding. John Moore's portrait of Tewkesbury and Laurie Lee's of Slad are well known, but Leonard Clark's of Cinderford and the edge of the Forest of Dean is equally one to savour.

Finally we have two experienced writers on country matters who lived for a while in Gloucestershire and brought a wider perspective to their reflections. One, Henry Warren focused on a small settlement on the Cotswold edge, the other H.J. Massingham, took in the whole stretch of the Cotswolds. They were professional writers.

Some of these writers lived most of their life within the county, others stayed only briefly, perhaps for a few years, and in Gilpin's case for just two days. This affected the way they wrote about landscapes and it is noticeable that for those brought up in the area, or living here for a long time, their landscapes were peopled. For them the visible landscape was a working and lived-in landscape, and it was not possible to separate place and people.

The authors wrote for different reasons—to fulfil a publisher's contract, to make some money, to express gratitude for their experiences of life here. Some were persuaded by friends to put in print their specialist knowledge and not all intended their work to be published. The later writers often drew on the earlier ones, Massingham on Gissing, Clark on Harvey, Jewson on Evans, Evans on Gibbs. They were mostly well-educated and more than half were Oxbridge men, but not all, and some were largely self taught through avid reading. Their styles differ, some is poetry, some is prose; some is gentle and courteous, some is critical and even acerbic. But it is all of high quality.

The writings span 180 years during which time many changes in the landscape occurred, although the massive disruption to the rural landscape caused by the Parliamentary Enclosures had passed. They wrote about different parts of Gloucestershire, giving their responses to what they saw both at the time and, in some cases, years before. What they have in common is an appreciation and love of their subject matter and an ability to see beyond the visible landscapes they are keen to describe. This is what sets them apart and gives distinction to their writing. They sought to discover the spirit of the place and as they did so they also conveyed to their readers how they viewed the landscape. From them we can learn much.

I. A VIEW FROM SYMONDS YAT LOOKING NORTH. GILPIN INTENDED TO CLIMB UP FROM HIS BOAT ON THE WYE FOR THIS VIEW BUT HEAVY RAIN PREVENTED HIM

2. LOWER LYDBROOK, FORMERLY A CENTRE OF HEAVY INDUSTRY

WILLIAM GILPIN

THE SEARCH FOR THE PICTURESQUE IN THE WYE VALLEY

Observations on the River Wye and South Wales, relative chiefly to Picturesque Beauty 1782–3

Through his series of five books of *Observations* …, William Gilpin gave his readers practical advice on how to look at landscapes, and where to find the views worth adapting and recording on their sketch-pad, or canvas.

Gilpin was born in 1724 into a happy, cultured home at Scaleby Castle, near Carlisle. Both at home and later at St Bees School he was encouraged to draw. He continued to do so, as a recreational activity, while an undergraduate at Queen's College, Oxford, at which time he also began to visit art collections. After ordination and a curacy at Irthington, not far from his home, he moved south, and in 1752 became Headmaster of Cheam School in Surrey. Here he worked for the next twenty-five years. He introduced gardening and business studies into the school curriculum and pioneered a system of punishments in which fines were substituted for corporal punishments—the fines being used for school improvements, such as books for the library and for building fives courts, or for charitable purposes in dole bread for the poor. During the long summer vacations he made sketching tours.

His lakeland upbringing had given him a love of wild, mountain scenery, and eighteenth century writers, such as Pope, Addison and Locke, had encouraged him to reject the ornate, regimented and sophisticated. So nature was to be contemplated as 'God's work of art'. In 1768 he published *An Essay on Prints*, which gave guidance to the layman on print collecting, and he began to apply the techniques of art criticism to viewing landscapes and to look for 'that kind of beauty that would look well in a picture'.

In 1777 he was presented with the living of Boldre in the New Forest, a large and, at that time, lawless parish, with its poachers, smugglers and squatters. He remained there for the rest of his life and died in 1804. He systematically visited all of his congregation, preached simple country sermons, and concentrated especially on the children of the parish. He had a school built for them, and to help fund it Gilpin decided to publish his *Observations*. The first, on the Wye valley, described a tour made in 1770, and was chosen because of its relatively small size and fewer prints, which made it easier to publish. In it he began to teach this new way of looking at landscape—the picturesque view.

The picturesque view was not an actual view but one that was composed. It was a creation rather than a reproduction. The elements of the view were copied from nature and then arranged into a harmonious whole. The finished sketch, or painting, caught the 'spirit and truth' of the original. One consequence was that later tourists, who took Gilpin's prints with them on their travels, could rarely find the exact viewing point. He said there should be one leading subject which characterised the view, with other features playing a supporting role. Usually the view had three parts—foreground, middle distance, and background—which could either blend in with one another, or be sharply defined. The foreground had depth and width and laid the foundation for the picture. It was rich, dark and forceful, such as a large gnarled tree, or a rugged rock outcrop. The middle distance contained the leading subject, such as a waterfall, or ruined castle, which was strongly lit. Light and shade characterised the middle distance. The background was tender and misty. Although cattle and ruins were allowed, cottages and peasants were not. It was a largely uninhabited landscape, unspoilt by the civilising hand of man. For a sublime view special lighting was necessary, such as was associated with storm clouds, or mist, or sunrise, or especially sunset with light slanting in through trees. Cloudy conditions were also highly valued. The view was to stimulate the imagination and to encourage the observer to examine the scene. 'The painter should endeavour to please the eye, he should aim to make the country he carries us through such as we would wish to inhabit, or at least to examine'. The eye was led on by a winding river, or perhaps by small silhouette figures pointing to something hidden and unknown. The picturesque view had a low vantage point, so it was framed by side screens, like the wings of a stage. It was a 'humble' view, in contrast to the aerial, oblique angle, estate-enhancing engravings of Jan Kip, which had been used to illustrate Sir Robert Atkyns' *Ancient and Present State of Gloucestershire* of 1712.

Gilpin's concept of the picturesque resonated with the tastes of those people who had received a classical education, who had followed the standard Grand Tour of Europe, and had seen or collected paintings by the seventeenth-century French and Italian artists such as Claude Lorrain, Nicolas Poussin and Salvator Rosa.

The original journey was made in the summer of 1770. Gilpin travelled from Kingston in Surrey, via Reading and Oxford. Then he crossed the Cotswolds, which he described as downs. Around Northleach the downs were enclosed by stone walls, which he thought were the most offensive separation of property. Three views impressed him as he moved through Gloucestershire, the pleasant view of the Windrush valley with its pollarded willows and luxuriant vegetation near the Barringtons, the noble view above Dowdeswell over the Severn Valley to the Malverns near the eleventh milestone from Gloucester—a view now dominated by Cheltenham—and the view from outside Gloucester's west gate, over the grazed meadows and sloping woods to the hills beyond.

At Ross the final plans for the journey down the Wye were made, and a covered boat with three oarsmen was hired. On the next day, soon after the journey commenced, rain set in. This gave 'a veil of obscurity' but contributed to the 'gloomy grandeur of the scene'. The rain prevented the anticipated landing at Goodrich to take in the view from the castle and also the walk from Coldwell Rocks over to New Weir (Symonds Yat) to see the reported noble river views [fig. 1]. The 'neat and pleasant' town of Monmouth was reached after sunset.

The next day was sunny and Gilpin decided to continue the journey by boat, rather than by chaise as originally intended. Landings were made at Tintern Abbey, where he was shocked by the wretched condition of the beggar guides, and then at Piercefield for the garden tour, from which he walked into Chepstow as the tide was out and there was insufficient water to re-embark. The 'whole valley was such a display of picturesque scenery that it is beyond any commendation', he wrote. Within it he identified three grand views and several others having very picturesque qualities.

With fifty-six rough sketches and his notes of the journey, Gilpin prepared a manuscript for limited circulation. Sketching was easier on a smooth running boat than in a jolting carriage. He received favourable comments on the manuscript and so based the 1782 publication on it.

There is an extensive view westward from the churchyard at Ross. But Gilpin immediately stated that, although admired, the view was not picturesque. The viewpoint is too high, the scenery too fragmented and it is without unifying character.

The first grand view is at Goodrich. The 'lofty banks and mazy course' of the Wye provided the three parts—the water is the foreground or area, the steep valley sides the two side screens, and the front screen in the distance results from the meandering course of the river. The valley sides vary in height and slope angle, in their covering of rock, grass and trees, and in their buildings. At Goodrich the view is simple, with a wide sweep of the river leading the eye onward and with the ruined castle crowning the hill as the dominant subject. A few trees in the foreground would have contributed to the quality of the view, but in those days no trees were allowed at the water's edge for navigational reasons.

The next view of great grandeur has the spire of Ruardean church as its focus. Here the valley sides are wooded and perspective is given by a long, straight stretch of river, with diversity provided by stone quarries on the right and an iron furnace on the left. The smoke from the charcoal burning for these furnaces gave a thin veil over the valley sides and, wrote Gilpin, 'unites these with the sky', an expression Wordsworth used later in his *Lines above Tintern*. In contrast to the tranquility and gentleness of most of the scenery, Lydbrook was a place of busy industrial activity, with boats being loaded with coal for transport up and down river [fig 2]. Near Whitchurch he noticed the large blocks of rock scattered over the hillsides. These are rocks fractured from the outcrop of Quartz Conglomerate and brought down the slopes by periglacial solifluction.

At New Weir (Symonds Yat), Gilpin recorded his second grand view. Here the valley sides are very steep, and rugged cliffs appear through the trees. Smoke rose from a forge hidden in a small cluster of houses, and the turbulence of water passing the rapids contributed to the impact the scenery made on him.

3. THE RUINS OF TINTERN ABBEY FROM THE LEFT BANK OF THE WYE

Ploughed land and corn fields were not desired for the picturesque view. Pastureland with flocks of sheep and herds of cattle were conceived to be more natural and attractive to the artist, and the meadows and low hills below Monmouth, seen against the white sails of river boats, were very picturesque.

At Tintern was the grandest view of the whole voyage. Here the ruins of the secluded abbey, 'site of medieval meditation', were set in a bend of the river [fig. 3]. The close up inspection of the weathered stone work, partly covered in ivy, lichen, moss and other plants, and of the elaborate structure of the interior of the abbey, were additional delights. Gilpin preferred the view from the road to that from the river and made a comment, subsequently picked up by critics of the picturesque, that the whole scene would have been more attractive if the hard lines of the well preserved gable ends of the abbey church had been broken by the judicious use of a mallet! Below Tintern, the tidal effects were detrimental to the scenery. The silt suspended in the water restricted reflection, and the river banks were sludgy at low tide [fig. 4].

Piecefield, the last stopping point, was a well-known and popular landscaped estate. Walks had been laid out by Valentine Morris, a wealthy owner of Antiguan sugar plantations, to allow the visitor access to a succession of view points, to a grotto, a cave and to carefully positioned seats. But to Gilpin, it was too embellished with plantings of shrubs and flowers to be natural and informal. It was, however, an eighteenth century beauty spot and open to the public, or rather the discerning public, on Tuesdays and Fridays.

4. TIDAL STRETCH OF THE WYE NEAR LANCAUT.

Gilpin's book became very influential and by 1800 eight boats were available for hire at Ross for the Wye tour [fig. 5]. The price was one and a half guineas from Ross to Monmouth and three guineas for the whole forty mile journey from Ross to Chepstow. It had become an essential part of the education of all 'who aspire to the reputation of elegance, taste, and fashion'. Many prints, drawings and paintings were available from shops, besides the selection in Gilpin's *Observations* ... [fig. 6]. Visitors took the book, or a selection of prints, with them to help them hunt out the views and then they produced their own illustrations, rather like today's holiday-makers who photograph scenes identified from tourist brochures. Apart from sketch pads and artists' materials, note books and guides, maps, and possibly Cowper's poems, an important aid in the search for the picturesque was the Claude glass. This was a small plano-concave mirror in a case. It gave a true reflection of the foreground but reduced the surroundings. Tinted glass was also used to give the mellow brown colours associated with the classical seventeenth-century landscape painters. The tourist held up the mirror to view the reflection of the landscape behind him, and when satisfied with the picturesque qualities of the view, turned round to enjoy it! Overnight accommodation was available at Ross and at Monmouth, and the standard picnic spots were at Symonds Yat and Tintern, where two hour stops were made. After 1828 the tour could be made by road, and after 1876 by rail. In the latter case, there were moonlight excursions. However, it was during the Napoleonic Wars, when continental travel was prevented, that the tour became most popular.

5. LOWER REDBROOK TINPLATE WORKS, MID-NINETEENTH CENTURY. NOTICE THE BOAT TAKING
PASSENGERS ON THE WYE TOUR

c. William Gilpin: 'Tintern-abbey from the land-side'

d. William Gilpin: 'View of Tintern-abbey from the road'

e. William Sawrey Gilpin: View of Tintern Abbey from the road

f. Francis Jukes: View of Tintern Abbey from the road

6. GILPIN'S ORIGINAL SKETCH OF TINTERN ABBEY IS SHOWN TOP LEFT

7. THE SETTING FOR WORDSWORTH'S *LINES ABOVE TINTERN*

Gilpin's scheme was soon regarded as too rigid, inflexible and mechanistic. It was caricatured by William Combe in *Dr Syntax*, and Gilpin himself recognised the monotony of the terms—high, low, steep, woody, rocky, noble—used in his book.

With the rise of romanticism, landscape appreciation again changed. This is clearly demonstrated in Wordsworth's *Lines above Tintern*, written in the summer of 1798. Wordsworth walked the Wye valley rather than travelling by boat. Two days before setting out, he dined with the Revd Richard Warner, who was Gilpin's curate at Boldre. He took Gilpin's book with him, and the similarities and differences between the two publications are instructive. The feature in the foreground for Wordsworth is a dark sycamore tree, in the lit middle distance are the steep and lofty cliffs, and the landscape of the far distance merges with the quiet of the sky [fig. 7]. But the billowing clouds of smoke from the industrial sites have become wreaths of smoke from the fire of a vagrant, or hermit. The landscape is largely uninhabited, woods are houseless, cottages are lost in woods and copses, and signs of farming are restricted to hedgerows—lines of sportive wood run wild, and orchards in which the fruit is green. In fact green is the dominant colour. So industry has gone, hovels have gone, and the lonely hermit is introduced. Sounds become more significant—the murmur of the river water, the silence of the trees—and memories and moods begin to influence the appreciation of the scenery. The title is *Lines above Tintern*, not 'at Tintern', the ruined abbey is no longer the focus.

The Wye valley is still a popular tourist area and many of the visitors who photograph the scenery are equally influenced by guide books and brochures in the selection of view points—and they are therefore unconsciously indebted to William Gilpin and the principles he expounded.

Places to visit: Ross church for the view west over the Wye. Goodrich Castle. Lower Lydbrook, an old industrial site. Symonds Yat for the view from Yat Rock and from the banks of the Wye. Monmouth for old hotels. Tintern Abbey and also the view from Devil's Pulpit. Wintour's Leap. Lancaut church. Piecefield for its landscaping. Chepstow and its castle.

(NB. The county boundary follows the centre of the Wye at Tintern and above and below Symonds Yat.)

John Keble

Signs of the Spiritual in the Natural Scenery around Fairford

The Christian Year, 1827

Several notable people who have had a major influence on the Church in England were born in Gloucestershire. These include William Tyndale, whose aim as a translator was to make the Bible accessible even to the ploughboy, George Whitefield, the eighteenth century evangelist who could hold the attention of crowds of ten thousand people without a modern amplification system, and John Keble. Keble was born in Fairford in 1792. His father was the vicar of Coln St Aldwyns, but chose to live in his own house in Fairford some two and a half miles away. The house was then called Court Close and is now Keble House [fig. 8]. The family roots were in the area, as can be seen by several monuments in Southrop Church, and one ancestor, Richard Keble, was a sixteenth century lord of the manor of Eastleach Turville [fig. 9]. Both John and his younger brother Thomas were taught at home by their father and both gained scholarships to Corpus Christi College, Oxford. John took a double first, in Mathematics and Classics, and then moved to Oriel College as a tutor and examiner. He was ordained in 1815. Then, until he became vicar of Hursley in Hampshire in 1836, he lived mainly in the family house at Fairford, though for a while at Oriel and for two years in the rectory at Southrop. He was curate at the Eastleach churches [fig. 10] from 1816 to 1825, curate at Southrop from 1823 to 1825, and from 1826 helped his father at Coln St Aldwyns. With his gentle, rather shy and diffident manner, Keble did not find pastoral work easy. The local farmers were quarrelsome and farmworkers oppressed and starving, like the unemployed weavers in his brother Thomas' parish at Bisley, and some of his university friends were amazed 'at the first man in Oxford burying himself in a tiny Gloucestershire parish simply to minister to the souls of a handful of rustics'.

On his walks or rides to conduct church services, or to visit parishioners, Keble continued to compose verse, a practice he had begun at Oxford in 1819. These verses were based largely on the Bible readings listed in the Prayer Book for each Sunday and Feast Day in the church calendar, but also on the writings of the early Fathers and the seventeenth century English Divines, and occasionally on his observations of the natural world. The allusions are often obscure and it is not easy to follow his train of thought. He

8. KEBLE HOUSE, FORMERLY COURT CLOSE, FAIRFORD, THE BIRTH PLACE
OF JOHN KEBLE

9. KEBLE'S BRIDGE AT EASTLEACH. ALTHOUGH JOHN KEBLE OFTEN CROSSED IT, THE BRIDGE IS NOT
NAMED AFTER HIM BUT AFTER ONE OF HIS ANCESTORS WHO LIVED HERE

10. THE CHURCH OF ST MICHAEL AND ST MARTIN, EASTLEACH MARTIN WITH THE CHURCH OF ST ANDREW, EASTLEACH TURVILLE AMONG THE TREES BEHIND. KEBLE SERVED AS CURATE TO BOTH CHURCHES FROM 1816 TO 1825

knew and admired Wordsworth, and like him drew inspiration from nature. Later, when elected Professor of Poetry at Oxford 1831–1841, his lectures in Latin included a number on the significance of pastoral poems. He intended to work on his own poems for the rest of his life but news of their existence was leaked out by friends of his sisters and in response to the wishes of his elderly father, a small, plain, anonymous volume entitled *The Christian Year* was published by Parkers of Oxford in 1827.

The poems conformed to the tastes of the day and, since they were devotional, appealed to a broad spectrum of Christians. In a few weeks a second edition was required, and no less than ninety-two editions were published in Keble's lifetime and one hundred and fifty-eight editions before the copyright ran out in 1873. David Newsome in his book *Godliness and Good Learning*, on influential Victorian Headmasters, writes that 'beside his Bible and his classical authors, the early Victorian intellectual was most conspicuously influenced by five literary works, which did more to form his ideas, quicken his emotions and inspire his politics than any other influence of a cultural or philosophic kind.' The five works were Butler's *Analogy*, Wordsworth's poems, Scott's novels, Coleridge's *Aids to Reflection*, and Keble's *Christian Year*. Wordsworth thought *The Christian Year* so good he wished he had written it so that he could rewrite it and make it better, while Housman thought it could be admired by an atheist.

Some of the poems have become well known hymns such as 'New every morning is the love' and 'Blessed are the pure in heart', but most no longer appeal, partly because of their style and language, and partly because of their unfamiliar content. They have been assessed by some critics as more an intellectual exercise than a matter of inspiration, technical but tone deaf, correct but not fresh, suitable for analysis rather than for singing. Keble himself regretted their popularity, thinking that they set him up as a better man than he was and that they rather exposed his private thoughts. He referred to them as 'pottery', meant for plain matter-of-fact people. However, the royalties the book brought him enabled the rebuilding of the church at Hursley. In this chapter the focus is on Keble's approach to nature.

The landscape of the area between Fairford and Eastleach is an open one of low relief, but high enough to command extensive views to the east over the Isis, or upper Thames valley to the far distant Berkshire Downs. There is, therefore, as in East Anglia, a broad expanse of sky and the changing cloud patterns are conspicuous and impressive, especially when walking in the area. Keble frequently mentions clouds and sky in his poems. 'The glorious sky embracing all is like the Maker's love'. The rainbow backed by storm clouds reminded him that just as the darkest, gloomiest places may be lit up so brightly, so the gleam of faith shown by one parishoner illuminated what would have been a depressing pastoral round. The most striking use of clouds is in the poem for Ascension Day, where the fiery golden rim of a cloud hiding the sun is likened to an angel's pavement. As he says in one of his published lectures, nature provides a rich wealth of similes 'whereby a pious mind may supply and remedy its powerlessness of speech'.

11. KEBLE OFTEN WALKED HERE BY THE RIVER LEACH ON HIS PASTORAL VISITS

12. WILLOWS BY THE RIVER COLN

The skylark, still found in the area, is the most frequently mentioned bird in his poems, soaring in flight and in song, even in gloomy weather. The robin, 'sweet messenger of calm decay', provides the subject for an autumn hymn and the evening song of the blackbird and the mournful notes of the turtle-dove gave inspiration for others.

His botanical interest, which was developed as an undergraduate, continued throughout his life. The local woods such as Eastleach Grove, now cleared, were visited in search of Anemone *pulsatilla*, the pasque flower, in the company of young friends he was tutoring at Southrop during the university vacations. Several impressionable young men spent time with him here studying Greek, reading, talking and walking in the surrounding countryside. Keble was impressed by the prodigality of nature, realised he said, when considering 'the wealth of flowers scattered in every nook and corner, of infinite and most delightful variety, whose colours and features nevertheless no single human being will ever enjoy'. The snowdrop 'the firstborn of the year's delight' symbolised the news of Easter. Violets reminded him of joy and hope and perhaps significantly he gave his wife Charlotte a bunch of violets picked along the Gloucester road on their wedding day in October 1835. Both the Rivers Coln and Leach [fig. 11] were bordered by willows drooping over the water and bending in the breeze, and he notes how the soft green colour follows the vernal red of the stem tips [fig. 12]. The primrose is mentioned in another poem as requiring the moisture of a shady path but also bursts of light [fig. 13]. He learned lessons for old age from the falling leaves of autumn and the fresh growth of spring. He took seriously the words of Jesus 'Consider the lilies of the field' and expressed them in these lines:—

13. 'NOR VAINLY SMILES ALONG THE SHADY WAY
THE PRIMROSE IN HER VERNAL NEST'

For ye could draw the admiring gaze
Of Him who worlds and hearts surveys:
Your order wild, your fragrant maze,
He taught us how to prize.

He was a keen gardener, both at Fairford and Southrop, and then more continuously at Hursley. Writing in the early days in Hampshire, he looked forward to the time when the garden which was then 'cabbaged, beaned and mustard and cressed would be rosed, pinked and strawberried'.

He rarely commented on urban life, which in the early nineteenth century was often associated with smokey surroundings and noisy, busy, dreariness, but even here he is optimistic: 'But Love's a flower that will not die for lack of leafy green'.

When reviewing classical poetry in his Oxford lectures, he distinguished between those poets concerned with celebrating the affairs of men and those seeking solace in rural life and the study of nature. Of the latter, some like Lucretius, inquired into nature's inner truth, others like Virgil enjoyed her charms. Keble sympathised with Virgil. Tradition has it that some of his poems were written in the churchyard at Southrop, beneath one of the yew trees, though his preferred place of writing was in the sitting room using the mantlepiece as a desk. But whether in the valley of the Leach, or on holiday in the Lake District or on the Dorset coast, his enjoyment of nature was always enhanced by the insight it gave into

Christian truth. He looked beyond visible things to their sacred and moral meanings, or as Pusey put it 'he saw the natural world as an emblem of the spiritual'.

The Christian Year brought fame to this gifted country vicar and contributed to his strong influence on the Oxford Movement. This Movement in time made its impact on the Gloucestershire landscape in the new churches and rectories built in some of the poorer woollen areas of the Cotswolds around Bisley. Oakridge (1837), Bussage (1846), France Lynch (1857) and the rebuilt church at Stinchcombe (1855), are examples of the type of architecture thought appropriate for the High Church style of worship. Gable crosses and triple lancet windows with a hood mould over them symbolised the unity of the Godhead. Stone carvings of early church leaders are also characteristic. Of those undergraduates Keble tutored at Southrop, Isaac Williams became curate at Windrush and later helped Thomas Keble at Bisley, living at Over Court and then at Stinchcombe writing poetry, sermons and commentaries and Sir George Prevost, who after a curacy at Bisley, became perpetual curate of Stinchcombe, building the manor house, rectory and school there, and then later Archdeacon of Gloucester.

Keble died in March 1866 and was buried in the churchyard at Hursley. In May of that year plans were made to raise money for a lasting memorial and in 1869 Keble College, Oxford was opened in his memory. But it was for *The Christian Year* that most people in Victorian times remembered John Keble.

Places to visit: The walk over the fields from Southrop to Eastleach Martin and Turville is a pleasant one, particularly in spring when the daffodils by the Leach near Keble's Bridge are in flower. St Andrew's Church, Eastleach Turville displays a copy of The Christian Year. *St Peter's Church, Southrop has a magnificent Norman font discovered by John Keble when restoration work was being undertaken. The nineteenth century Tractarian churches around Bisley, as referred to previously, are worth a visit and are situated on the sides of scenic valleys. All Saints, Bisley was the hub of the Oxford Movement on the Cotswolds.*

14. ST PETER'S CHURCH, UPPER SLAUGHTER, WHERE FRANCIS WITTS WAS RECTOR
FROM 1808 TO 1854

15. OVER BRIDGE, GLOUCESTER. WITTS WATCHED ITS CONSTRUCTION IN THE 1820S ON
HIS VISITS TO GLOUCESTER

Francis Witts

A Meticulous Diarist recording changes in early nineteenth-century Gloucestershire

The Diary of a Cotswold Parson 1820–1852, edited by David Verey

Francis Witts became Rector of Upper Slaughter in 1808 [fig. 14], when at the age of 25 he succeeded his uncle the Reverend Ferdinando Tracy Travell. He continued in this position until his death in 1854. From 1814 he was also Vicar of Stanway. He was well-to-do, having been blessed, he wrote, 'with ample provision of earthly comfort'. He frequently dined with the gentry, not only of this part of the Cotswolds, but of a much wider area. He was a magistrate with many attendant duties and this entailed frequent journeys to court in Gloucester. He was also responsible for making some of the arrangements for the Three Choirs Festival. He was knowledgeable about farming matters and took pride in his own estate.

His diaries, which ran into ninety notebooks, have been edited, and the published selection relates to his life in the county at large, rather than to his pastoral work in Upper Slaughter or to family affairs, though reference is made to a few of the latter. He lived in the rectory, now the Lords of the Manor Hotel, and in fact he bought the lordship of the manor from Lord Sherborne in 1852.

During the thirty years covered by the diaries, huge changes in transport occurred. Witts usually rode on horseback in the early years, and did so until a nasty fall in 1835 severely shook him. He also travelled by a variety of horse-drawn carriages. He mentions open, gig, fly, phaeton, chariot and postchaise, and for more distant travel he used the stagecoach services. Interestingly the toll board at Butterrow refers to the tolls charged for several of these different types of carriage. He names the stage-coaches he used, the Regulator, the Novelty and the Magnet. An average speed for these was ten miles per hour and he records how in 1835 he could leave the rectory after an early breakfast, catch the Oxford coach at Stow at 6 a.m., then at Oxford transfer to the London coach and reach the coach office in London's Oxford Street at 4 p.m. A few years later in 1839, he caught the Magnet at Northleach at 8 a.m. for Maidenhead. Here the coach was loaded on to a railway truck while he took his seat in a first class compartment and so travelled by GWR to Paddington. Then with new horses the coach continued to Oxford Street.

Roads figure prominently in the early years of the diary, and especially when they had been recently improved. The growth of fashionable Cheltenham demanded better access from the London direction, so the steep and dangerous approach from the south-east through Dowdeswell was avoided by a new gentle course north of Sandywell Park, opened in 1824. From 1825 the turnpike from Bath via Painswick followed an elegant line along the hillside, through the beech woods above Prinknash. In 1823 the steep gradients on the old road from Winchcombe were avoided by skirting Cleeve Hill, and the approach from Gloucester took the Lansdown Road from 1832. There was also a new turnpike road from Cirencester opened in 1826. Occasionally Witts comments on the conditions of the road surfaces, or their width, or the snow and ice he faced in winter, but most references are to improvements. Of special interest to him were the new bridges over the Severn. Mythe Bridge at Tewkesbury, which was opened in 1825, and Haw Bridge, a few miles downstream, were both viewed, and he visited Over Bridge at Gloucester [fig. 15] on several occasions during its construction. The latter was at the time the widest single-span bridge in the country and Witts was greatly impressed by its graceful form. Pre-cut sandstone blocks from quarries in the Forest of Dean were brought by barge, and under Telford's supervision and with a large labour force, the bridge was completed in 1829 at a cost of £43,000. It continued in use for main road traffic until 1974 and is now preserved by English Heritage.

Telford was also responsible for bringing to completion the protracted construction of the Gloucester-Sharpness Canal in 1827. The Canal, which was designed to allow shipping to avoid the navigation problems of the tidal Severn, was begun in 1794. With its large dock basin and capacious warehouses, the Canal made a major contribution to Gloucester's prosperity. Details of items handled by the port are given. Salt and iron manufactures were exported, and Irish grain, Canadian timber, Welsh slate and wines from Spain and Portugal were imported. One of the problems of canal transport was ice in a severe winter. This affected areas far from the canal side and Witts quotes the price of coal at Stow at 50s. (£2.50) per ton in February 1830, whereas the normal price was 28s. (£1.40) per ton.

In the later years of the diary travel by rail is discussed. In July 1840 he showed his wife around the unfinished railway station at Lansdown, Cheltenham and the locomotives and carriages there. He always travelled first class and his servant second class. Rail travel was relatively speedy, apart from on embankments, and often bumpy. As early as 1824 he mentions the possible use of steampower when referring to the new horse-drawn railroad built to carry coal from Stratford to Moreton-in-Marsh. On his visits to Lydney Park he observed the Severn-Wye Railroad and others in the Forest of Dean by which coal, iron, stone and timber were transported to the Severn or Wye ports such as Lydney and Lydbrook. One novel method of transport that captured his imagination was a four-wheeled chair pulled from Gloucester to Cheltenham by two kites, strung together and driven by a strong south-west wind.

The leisurely speed of horse-drawn coach or carriage enabled passengers to view the surrounding countryside as they travelled and there are frequent comments in the

16. VIEW FROM FROCESTER HILL LOOKING SOUTH-WEST,
A VIEW WITTS MENTIONS IN HIS DIARY

diary on the best viewpoints. So the reader is taken to Brookthorpe and Highnam for views of Gloucester Cathedral, to the terrace at Prinknash and the high points along the escarpment, such as Painswick Beacon, Frocester Hill [fig. 16], or Uley Bury, for the view west over the Severn valley. Coopers Hill provided a view northward and Sharpness Point overlooked the lower Severn. From Lydney Park and Hardwick Court there were fine easterly views.

Most farmland was enclosed by now and the fertility of the Severn Valley with its rich dairy pastures, apple orchards and cornfields pleased him, as did the productive cottage gardens at Blakeney. He did not subscribe to the popular opinion of the Cotswolds held by some of his friends—bleak hills, stone walls and horrors, though William Cobbett writing in 1825 described it as miserable country, 'any thing so ugly I have never seen before'. Witts gladly showed his visitors its warm valleys, rich meadows, luxuriant hedges and fine autumnal foliage. He noticed the effect of prolonged drought on crops, especially on turnips, oats and barley, and was interested in new field crops such as a particular clover, once a garden flower, but now cultivated as a productive and nutritious fodder crop. He was also interested in farm livestock and records attending the sale of Southdown sheep and Devon cattle at Temple Guiting, following the death there of George Talbot in 1836.

Witts understood the concept of the picturesque and described the clothing valleys of Chalford and Woodchester as such. On his ride through the beech woods near Cranham he noted the newly-built thatched cottages at Buckholt, so reminiscent of those in Repton's Red Books, which were attracting many visitors from Cheltenham. Then, at a later date in his diary, he records the grand view of the Severn estuary and the country beyond, seen from the Roman camp in Lydney Park. Here he also comments on the effects of light and shade in the groves, on the varied forms of the native trees and on the rugged combination of massive rocks and gnarled yews in the Scowles, the ancient iron mines in the north of the park. These were subjects well suited to the landscape painter he thought. Mature trees gave him pleasure and many species are mentioned—in the Forest of Dean, Spanish chestnut, oak, ash, lime, maple, birch, yew and holly, but not conifers; on the Cotswolds beech, and black poplar with mistletoe growing on its branches by the Severn. The botanical interest shown by his son Edward prompted several entries. Of special interest was the discovery on some steep banks on the Rectory (later Home) Farm of the rare perfoliate pennycress—*Thlaspi perfoliatum*. Witts mentions several other sites where the plant was to be found, and it is still to be seen in a few places on the Cotswolds. During his student days at Oxford, Edward made frequent visits in search of wild flowers to such habitats as Cirencester Park, Sandywell Woods and Cranham Woods, to the approval of his doting father.

Changes were also occurring in the old county town and more so in the new spa town. When in Gloucester for Court or Church duties, Witts normally stayed either with his mother-in-law in Wellington Parade off London Road, or at the Bell Inn in Southgate, or with the Howells at Prinknash. The Bell was the meeting place for Tories. Whigs met at the King's Head Inn in Westgate, which was next to St Nicholas House, and from which the assembled magistrates walked to the court. In the 1820s a fashionable area was being developed around Spa Road in association with some saline springs, and Christ Church, Brunswick Road, was built in 1822 to serve this genteel suburb. Port activities stimulated housing development in Hempstead in the 1830s, and a little later came the growth of a large and poor district along the Tewkesbury Road. Witts attended many services in the Cathedral and was well aware of the disadvantage of sitting behind the massive Norman pillars! He comments on the new monuments in the cathedral to the Revd Richard Raikes, brother of the founder of Sunday schools (1823), to Sir George Onesiphorus Paul, the prison reformer (1825), to Dr Edward Jenner (1825) and to the gaoler Cunningham (1836). In the first years of the diary Gloucester was still the social centre of the county and Cheltenham was then described as 'a little country town not yet a public place'.

It soon became 'a luxurious and straggling resort of fashion', 'interesting and exciting', and Witts chronicles its speculative expansion during the late 1820s and 1830s. For a time it was the most rapidly growing town in Britain. Witts was born in Cheltenham in 1783 in a house adjoining the George Inn yard in the High Street, a site now occupied by Marks and Spencer, and his mother later lived at 2, Belle View. He visited each area of new building, first Lansdown Parade (1828), then the slow construction of Pittville, a planned new town, then Suffolk Square and Lansdown Crescent and Villas, and finally the layout of the Bayshill estate. Most houses were described as handsome, spacious and elegant, signifying affluence. He walked to the spas and assessed the company, 'speculating matrons, chaperoning fair and elegant but slenderly endowed nymphs with taper waists, and elderly bachelors from the banks of the Ganges with injured livers and bilious complexions, smiling their approbation', comments that were gentler and warmer than

17. MONTPELLIER PUMP
ROOM, CHELTENHAM

Cobbett's of 1826: 'To places like this come all that is knavish and all that is foolish and all that is base; gamesters, pickpockets, and harlots; young wife hunters in search of rich and ugly and old women, and young husband hunters in search of rich and wrinkled or half-rotten men … a place to which East India plunderers, West India floggers, English tax-gorgers, together with gluttons, drunkards and debauchees of all descriptions, female as well as male, resort at the suggestion of silently laughing quacks in the hope of getting rid of the bodily consequences of their manifold sins and iniquities'. The new copper dome on the Montpellier pump room (1826) impressed Witts [fig. 17], as did the splendour of the Pittville pump room on its completion in 1830. The layout of the shrubberies and shady walks at both Montpellier and Pittville was tasteful, and he did not begrudge the 1s. (5p) entrance fee to the walks at Pittville. The mean buildings of the Sherborne or Imperial Spa did not satisfy him, though its walks were shady and pleasant, and he welcomed the construction of the impressive Queen's Hotel (1838) on its site.

Apart from his numerous journeys to Gloucester and Cheltenham, he frequently visited friends for dinner. He was a great diner out. He did not care for late travel in the winter darkness but still accepted invitations for such meals. Visits were made to other clergy—the Astons at Wood Stanway, the Prices at Coln St Denis, the Warnefords at Bourton-on-the-Hill, the Baillies at Great Rissington, the Leighs at Broadwell and the Vavasours at Stow. Fellow magistrates, Bathurst at Lydney Park, Lloyd Baker at Hardwick Court and Waller at Farmington, and other friends and neighbours such as the Reades at Oddington, the Hastings at Daylesford, the Chamberlaynes at Maugersbury and especially the Howells at Prinknash also welcomed him for dinner. Sometimes he comments on the houses but more often on the grounds. Many of these were described as tasteful but he was aware that tastes change. So at Westbury mention is made of the formal garden, canals, yew hedges and the statue of Neptune; at Matson House the canal, bowling green and terrace are noted; at Temple Guiting a new style was being developed with a grotto and plantations; and at Hardwick Court, where the flat ground again gave limited scope, there was a hermitage, root house, greenhouse and aviary, and rocks had been brought in for a rockery. The combination of tree planting and sheets of water at Daylesford, Sezincote and Northwick Park, 'drest grounds', indicated another development, as did the exotic trees, including oranges, in Lydney Park. Work in his own garden at Upper Slaughter [fig. 18] included planting evergreens and a shady walk of elms, the cultivation of vines, and a late entry refers to purchasing dahlias from Jessops' nursery in Cheltenham. The final years of the eighteenth century and the first half of the nineteenth century saw the change from the more formal Dutch style of garden, as at Westbury, to the landscaped garden, through the influence of such designers as Kent, Brown and Repton. Witts only mentions Repton but he is clearly aware of the trends in fashion seen in the gardens he visited.

On the appointment of his great friend Thomas Howell as Inspector of Factories, following the 1833 Factories Regulation Act, Witts travelled with him to Blockley. He describes the air of prosperity here, brought about by the silk industry, and the many fine buildings. The small stream provided the water power for six mills to spin into thread silk imported from Turkey and Bengal. This was then sold to manufacturers in Coventry. He noted that the mill owners were dissenters. Chipping Campden also had a silk mill, but Witts' interest here in this 'dull, clean, disused market town' with its market hall and older style architecture was chiefly the church and its marble monuments to the Hicks and Noel families.

The superior water power resources and easier access to coal supplies made the Stroud valleys more suitable than other parts of the Cotswolds for the woollen industry. The rivers here were deep blue from the dyes used and the mills dominated the valleys. But there was unrest among the weavers and some rioting over poor wages. Witts showed little sympathy for lawlessness and as a magistrate always applied the law with rigour.

18. VIEW OF THE GARDEN THROUGH THE FRONT DOOR OF WITTS' HOME, NOW THE LORDS OF THE MANOR HOTEL

Similarly, when reports were given to him of the suspicion of outside investment and the opposition to forest enclosure shown by the iron workers and coal miners in the Forest of Dean, his attitude was that they should be grateful for regular work and no local tax. He was fascinated by the heavy industry of the Forest seen on his visits to the Bathursts at Lydney Park. He writes, 'The principal forge which we passed in a gigantic grim mass of buildings, intersected by railway tracks, abounding in steam engines, resounded with the clang of ponderous hammers, the blast of giant bellows and similar impressive noises, now louder, now more suppressed, as the varied operations proceed'. At Parkend he saw one of the largest coal mines, where 100 miners were employed. With steam-powered winding gear coal was drawn from a depth of 600 feet.

Visits to Stanway to the vicarage, the church, or to Stanway House, where his mother often stayed, gave him the opportunity to watch the progress in the building of the new manor house at Toddington [fig. 19]. While the Tracy family continued living in the old house, of which only the ruined gateway remains, the new one was erected at great expense. The design of the front of the mansion was based on the tower and cloisters of Magdalen College, Oxford and one of the windows copied the west window of Tintern Abbey. Later in his diary he commented on another expensive development at Highnam, where Gambier Parry's estate was being improved and the new church built. Growing populations in Gloucester and Cheltenham and in the industrial areas of the Forest of Dean and the textile valleys around Stroud also required new churches. And in some more rural areas, the older parish churches were expanded with new aisles as at Little Rissington, Charlton Kings and his own church at Upper Slaughter. He appreciated the architectural beauty of the great wool churches at Cirencester, Northleach and Chipping Campden.

There was considerable interest in antiquities at the end of the eighteenth and beginning of the nineteenth centuries. Samuel Lysons had excavated several Roman villas, including the one at Woodchester, and at the Roman camp in Lydney Park [fig. 20] many coins, pottery and mosaics had been found. The ruins of Hailes Abbey and Llanthony Abbey attracted visitors, as did those at Sudeley Castle. Witts refers to each of them.

19. THE NEW
TODDINGTON MANOR

20. EXCAVATIONS AT THE ROMAN SITE IN LYDNEY PARK

Cryptic comments are given about the first impressions of places. For example, Coalpit Heath near Chipping Sodbury, was 'all out at the elbows'; Berkeley was 'a mean town'; and Cranham, which on the surface has 'the appearance of a peaceful innocent rural abode of good will and honest simplicity', had a population whose habits were 'thievish and gross'. Witts was a man of decided views! He was conscious of his position in society, whether administering justice, dining with the gentry, or as a breeder of fine cattle. He was concerned with status, although he welcomed the fact that people both of lower orders and of elegance attended the parish church in Cheltenham, where Francis Close was the preacher. He disapproved of young squires spending their time in fox hunting, or racing, or in the gay frivolities of Brighton or Cheltenham. He also disapproved of clergy hunting, although fishing was an acceptable pastime for them. The absence from their country seats of the landed gentry for the London season, or for a stay at the seaside, or for a rambling tour, seemed ill-advised to him.

Witts was a kindly man and his monument in the side chapel of Upper Slaughter Church describes him rather awkwardly as 'a friendly counsellor to all even of the humblest classes whom his unvarying gentleness encouraged to seek advice from him in their difficulties'. The published extracts from his meticulous diary do not give sufficient details to fairly assess his influence, but they do give an insight into an early nineteenth-century squarson's perception of the rapidly changing landscapes of Gloucestershire at this time. As he travelled around the county he was always looking for new developments and was confident of progress, but his perspective was inevitably from the upper middle class. Reading these extracts from his diary makes it difficult to imagine that they were not meant for publication.

Places to visit. Upper Slaughter for the Lords of the Manor Hotel (Witts' home) and church for his memorial. Gloucester for the Cathedral, Docks, Over Bridge, Wellington Parade and Spa Road. Cheltenham for Regency developments at Montpellier, Lansdown, Bayshill and Pittville. Tewkesbury for the Mythe Bridge. Highnam Church, Prinknash, Toddington, Lydney Park, Berkeley Castle. These are all places Witts visited and commented upon in his diary.

H.G. Nicholls

A Landscape of Industrial History in the Making

The Forest of Dean—An Historical and Descriptive Account, 1858

Henry George Nicholls was vicar of Holy Trinity Church, Drybrook [fig. 21] between 1847 and 1866. At the age of twenty-five, the same age as Francis Witts when he came to Upper Slaughter, Nicholls arrived from Trinity College, Cambridge. The contrast with Cambridge must have been immense. Drybrook was a large parish, it included Lydbrook until 1851, and very poor. While he was here he wrote three books, *Personalities of the Forest of Dean* (1863) and *Iron Making in Olden Times* (1866), as well as his main book considered here. He assembled information from 'personal observation and other sources public, private, legendary and local.' The principal documents were the papers of the Free Miners' Court 1668–1754, the manuscripts of George Wyrrall of Bicknor Court 1780, and the papers of Edward Machen, Deputy Surveyor of the Forest of Dean. The research involved much correspondence and travel, including visits to the Public Records Office in London and discussion with local clergy and employers. His primary concern, however, was with ministering to a large mining and industrial population and this included the building of two schools, at Hoarthorns and Woodside. One is amazed that he had the energy and initiative to tackle the research for his books. *The Forest of Dean* was the first published account of the area.

In working through the records of the Miners' Court, Nicholls noticed that there was a change in the surnames of the free miners attending Court, either as jurors, or with disputes. There was in particular a rise in Welsh names—Morgan, Williams, Watkins etc., and he reflected on the temperament of the people. Many had moved into the Forest from surrounding parishes, or from much further afield, to find employment and the space in which to graze their livestock. As squatters they had lived in primitive accommodation— low, drystone, windowless, turf-covered cabins, partly stone paved. From time to time these hovels were cleared from the Crown land so that, for example, Atkyns mentions some four hundred cabins knocked down and only six keepers houses left in the Forest in 1712. By the 1851 census, however, the population had risen to thirteen thousand. Nicholls noted the poverty and insularity of the early population. He quotes two writers on the

21. THE SETTING OF HOLY TRINITY CHURCH, DRYBROOK, WHERE NICHOLLS WAS VICAR

subject, 'a sort of robustic, wild people that must be civilised by good discipline and government' and 'nearly as wretched as anything now existing in Ireland', and adds that 'having been for so many generations an isolated and peculiar people, most of them are ignorant of the rest of the world and have of course a correspondingly exaggerated idea of their own importance'. He considered them suspicious, superstitious, excitable and fatalistic. But he was quick to recognise their independent spirit, their gratitude for help when it was given and their care for one another when in need. He never condoned their riotous behaviour in destroying enclosure boundaries, which would have restricted the grazing of their animals, or their robbery of grain boats on the Severn and wagons of corn going to Gloucester market when they were starving, but he understood the desperate plight that led to these events. What they chiefly lacked he writes was 'more generosity and candour towards strangers'. But by the time of his book, the effect of schooling, the dedicated ministry of the clergy, more effective organisation of poor relief and improved mining regulations, which obviated the need for interminable disputes and litigation, had brought improvements to the people. Cottages were now of two floors with upward of four rooms, clothes were no longer home made, and there were gardens—although after a day's work in the mine there was never much energy left for gardening. The women and children took responsibility for the cow, a few sheep that grazed in the forest, the pigs and geese.

The geological structure of the Forest of Dean is a synclinal basin, so the coal measures, which rest on beds of limestone and sandstone, dip towards the centre and are exposed around the inside of the rim. Earlier mining took place near the rim, where the seams were followed underground, and the later shaft mining was towards the centre of the basin. The coal seams occur in three groups. In the lower group the Coleford High Delf is the principal seam and its surface outcrop in the Coleford area is marked by a number of pools. The middle group includes the Rocky, Starkey and Lower Delf, names that often occur in old documents of mining around Park End. The upper group of relatively unimportant seams is found in the heart of the Forest. Nicholls records the evocative names of the eighteenth century mines—'The Stay and Drink' at Serridge, 'The Go on and Prosper' at Monmouth Hill, 'The Long Looked For' at Yorkley, and later, the 'Strip and At It'. As with iron mining, free miners applied to the Gaveller, the local crown official, at Coleford for the right of a 'gale' or mining area where they could work, and the regulations imposed by the Court of Mines determined the spatial area around each pit to be protected from other applicants. It extended for a radius of 100 yds in 1678, 300 yds in 1692, 500 yds in 1728 and 1,000 yds in 1754. Mines were shallow and flooding was a recurrent problem. The types of coal were classified by size into house coal, smiths' coal and lime coal, diminishing in size and cost in this order. Prices were agreed at the Miners' Court at the Speech House [fig. 22] and increased with distance from the pit. They were generally higher on the east side of the Forest. The first water wheel driven pump, which enabled deeper mining, was installed in 1754 and a steam engine was used here in 1766. Nicholls records the successive licensing of steam engines across the area.

The number of pits increased steadily, 90 were operational in 1787, 104 in 1841, 221 in 1856. Improved transport, by packhorse and then tramroads, enabled coal to be carried to the river ports—to Newnham for Gloucester, to Lydney, Pirton, Gatcomb and Bullo for south Gloucestershire beyond the Severn and to Lydbrook for Hereford and Monmouth, and so the market was expanded. There was also a market for coking coal in the iron industry at Cinderford after 1795.

In 1856 the ten leading collieries were mainly in the valleys of the Cannop and Soudley Brooks. They were Park End, Light Moor, Crump Meadow, Bix Slade, Nelson, Hopewell, Vallets Level, Bilson, Arthur and Edward and the New Strip and At It. By then stone walls had replaced the timber lining of shafts and the engraving in Nicholls' book of

22. THE SPEECH HOUSE

23. A FREE MINE IN WIMBERRY SLADE (1997)

the exemplary Light Moor Colliery near Cinderford shows four sets of winding gear, chimney stacks, engine houses and several railway tracks.

Coal mining in the Forest has left few visible remains. There are several colliery buildings, which have been put to alternative uses, but none of these existed in Nicholls' time. Most of the spoil heaps have gone and the remaining waste, which has been planted with trees, post dates the 1850s. However many old plateway lines are still recognisable with their stone slabs, with bolt holes where the iron plates were fixed and there are also stone embankments and stone shaft tops. For example, the plateway in Wimberry Slade goes past the stonework remains of the Hopewell Colliery. It also served a series of free mines and stone quarries. One or two free mines are still worked [fig. 23]. They last for a few years with their corrugated iron sheds, narrow rails, piles of pit props and coal fragments covering the ground around the gridles where the coal is graded, but once mining ceases the drifts are closed and traces soon go.

Iron ore is contained in the upper beds of the Carboniferous Limestone, in the Crease Limestone, which outcrops at the rim of the Forest just outside the coal measures. The quality and type of ore varies but generally miners regarded the ore from the east of the Forest to be superior to the western deposits. It has been mined at least from Roman times judging by the Roman artefacts in cinders at Bream. The Scowles (irregular trenches and caves) indicate these early workings. Mining went down to the water table, which in summer could be three hundred feet below the surface. The demand for Forest iron ore varied with the productivity of the iron-making industry and with its quality as compared to imported iron ore. In Nicholls' day it was again on the increase, 20 mines were licenced in 1841 and the number had risen to 50 by 1856. The principal mines then were Buckshaft and Westbury Brook in the east and Easter and Old Sling in the west of the Forest. Ore was transported by plateway, or in the case of Edge Hill on mule back. Hundreds of men were employed in the main mines and free miners worked their smaller scale pits.

The earliest permanent furnaces in the Forest in 1635 were located at Park End, Cannop, Lydbrook and Soudley. These were the King's Iron Works because they were Crown property. They were twenty-two feet square stone structures, with bellows driven by water wheels, and the bottle shaped cavities were charged with a mixture of charcoal, ore and cinders, the latter being the abundant and widespread waste from earlier workings. Linked to the furnaces were forges, where the pig iron was converted to iron bars for sale. Forges required more power for their hammers and so were downstream of the furnaces. The remains of the furnace at Gun's Mill dates from 1683 and this replaced an earlier one which produced cannons for Holland in 1629. An early coke blast furnace still stands at Whitecliff. The main iron works in 1850 were at Cinderford, Park End, Soudley, Lydbrook and Lydney and the general prosperity of Dean depended on the state of the iron industry.

Many of Nicholls' parishioners worked in the iron works or in the mines—red clothes and skin indicated iron miners, black clothes and skin indicated coal miners. Comparisons were made between the appearance of the nineteenth century iron miner and the fifteenth century miner's brass in Newland Church which shows his woollen cloak, leather breeches, candle, hod and mattock [fig. 24].

For details of the early iron industry Nicholls used not only the Wyrrall papers and those of the Miners' Court but also the Mushet papers (the Mushets were leading iron makers in the Forest) and Isaac Taylor's one inch map of Gloucestershire gave him the locations of furnaces and forges in 1777. He was very interested in the iron industry [fig. 25] and had been down in the mines. In 1866, the year of his death, he published a more extended investigation of *Iron Making in the Forest of Dean*. Surprisingly in neither work does he mention the noise, dust and smoke, nor the way in which the

24. THE MINER'S BRASS, ALL
SAINTS CHURCH, NEWLAND

25. DARK HILL IRONWORKS, NEAR COLEFORD

night sky was lit up with the glow from the furnaces, though he calls the Forest the 'Old Black Country' of Gloucestershire.

The typical Forest scenery in Nicholls' day was of young oak woodland less than fifty years old [fig. 26], enclosed by earth banks topped by gorse, hawthorn hedges, stone walls, or by post and rail fences. Many areas were scarred, 'disfigured' Nicholls calls it, by furnaces and collieries and poor quality buildings. There were several noteable trees from earlier plantings such as the 'King Charles Oaks' of 1670 and older named trees such as the Crad Oak at Sallow Vallets, Jack of the Yat at Serridge and the Newland Oak. Frequent inroads into the woodland had been made by windthrow, for example by a storm on the 18th February 1662 when a thousand oaks were uprooted; by ruthless felling, for example by Sir John Winter in 1667 when only two hundred oaks were said to have survived; and by the persistent removal of trees legally or otherwise for charcoal for the ironworks or pit props for coal mines, or fuel for the houses. Enclosure was designed to protect the young trees from grazing livestock and was unpopular with the commoners who owned cows, sheep and pigs. After 1667 a maximum of 11,000 acres could be enclosed at any one time and as soon as the trees were established the enclosures were opened and new land was taken in. Nicholls records in detail these phases. He made special use of the notes of Edward Machen, Deputy Surveyor, who managed the Forest from 1808 to 1854. These notes range over such matters as the incidence of late frost damage which was especially severe on larch, spruce and silver fir; the damage caused by the oak leaf roller moths that defoliated trees in May and covered them with their webs; and the effects of

26. OAK WOODLAND PLANTED *C*.1810. NOTICE THE STONE SLABS OF THE PLATEWAY LEADING TO AN EARLY COAL MINE

mice, both long- and short-tailed, which in 1814 destroyed the majority of young trees. Other documents gave him details of experiments with planting densities, the best age of transplanting trees, species choice, the most effective methods of bark removal and whether or not dead limbs should be cut from older trees.

Besides oaks other trees had been planted. Scots pine, maritime pine, Weymouth pine, larch and Spanish chestnut are mentioned, but oaks dominate with nine-tenths of the plantings. Despite the demand for charcoal in iron-making, oaks were primarily dedicated to ship timbers so wide spacing between trees allowed the branching necessary to produce the variety of shapes for different parts of the ship.

The Forest was a Norman hunting ground for deer and other game, and the various royal visits to Flaxley Abbey and St Briavels Castle were for this purpose. The population of fallow deer has fluctuated. In the king's forest they were protected, and when the tree growth of new enclosures gave them cover their numbers rose, though limits of 800 were imposed in 1612. But in Nicholls' time they were viewed as having a demoralising effect on the foresters through their inducement to poaching and by 1855 they had been eliminated. Although it had long been recognised that their grazing damaged young trees, it was the way they unsettled the habits of the people that caused their demise. Nicholls remarked that they were highly ornamental. They are again numerous today.

With regard to bird life in the woods Nicholls used the notes of Machen to record the general decline of the bird population in the first half of the nineteenth century when kites, hawks and ravens became scarce. For the north-east of the Forest his source was a Mr Gee of Mitcheldean. Here the picture was more optimistic and many species are recorded as abundant. Nightjars, woodpeckers, tits, water ousels, turtle-doves, willow wrens and buzzards are noted and snipe and bitterns were found at the Dam Pool [fig. 27] near the head of the Cinderford valley.

Mr Gee was also his source of information about the flora of the north-east Forest and a list is given of noteworthy or rarer plants in the various habitats of the Mitcheldean area and other scattered sites. Nicholls mentions the reputation of the Wye valley for flowers, with the walk from Ross to Chepstow being the most productive in botanical interest in the country. One senses that Nicholls was not a naturalist himself and had to rely on others for his information. He was happier quoting estimates of loads of timber, or numbers of trees planted, or acres of enclosed woodland.

The hilly terrain of the Forest and the streams and boggy areas in the valleys made road building difficult. There was a need for the transport of minerals and timber to the exporting ports along the Severn and the Wye and to the markets in these directions for which the early through routes were ill-suited. Nicholls mentions traces of three ancient roads, especially the Dean's Road at Blackpool Bridge with its pitched and paved surface, and also those at the Kymin and Littledean Woodside.

An Elizabethan silver coin found at Nailbridge and the Judges' Lodge at Mitcheldean indicated the route of the High Road from Mitcheldean to Coleford. There was another from Littledean to Coleford. These roads were maintained in the eighteenth century from funds obtained from the sale of timber and Nicholls gives details of the repairs. At a later

27. THE DAM POOL, NEAR CINDERFORD

date the revenue from tolls taken at the numerous toll gates paid for road maintenance and it is possible to assess the relative importance of the roads from the yields of these toll gates. He comments on the capacity of the inns at Mitcheldean to support travellers and on the many horse ponds along the roads, but also on the difficulty of travel in winter and the wretched state of the roads in bad weather.

For the transport of coal, iron ore and stone plateways or tramroads were built. These had rails of L-shaped iron plates bolted to stone slabs along which horse drawn wagons were pulled. There were two main tramroads, one on the west of Dean from Lydbrook to Lydney, laid by the Severn-Wye Railway Co. and the other on the east of Dean from Churchway Colliery to Bullo Pill, laid by the Bullo Pill Railway Co. From both lines branch lines were laid to the principal mines and the whole network gradually developed from 1809 to the 1850s. Nicholls records the various concessions from the Crown for these lines. He does not mention the broad gauge railway line from Gloucester to South Wales, which opened in 1851, but he does refer to the earlier requests for a railway in the area and to the 1855 broad gauge branch line from Lightmoor Colliery to Cinderford where it joined the spur from the South Wales line.

Nicholls was naturally interested in the Forest churches. The peripheral churches are old. The churches at Newland, Staunton, Mitcheldean and St Briavels have Norman or even Saxon features but within the Forest itself all the Anglican churches date from the nineteenth century. The needs of the growing population of miners' families aroused the concern of two local clergy, Revd P.M. Procter, Vicar of Newland and Revd H. Berkin, Curate of Mitcheldean. Both men visited crowded miners' cottages to read and explain scripture and then, through schoolrooms which doubled as chapels, larger groups of children and adults were taught. The Crown granted plots of land for church buildings and with many philanthropic gifts the following churches were consecrated, Christ Church, Berry Hill 1816, Holy Trinity, Drybrook 1817, St Paul's, Park End 1822, St John's, Cinderford 1844, and lastly Lydbrook Church 1850. Nicholls records the costs of each church, the principal donations, the seating capacity and the date, preacher and text of each consecration! He himself succeeded the Revd H. Berkin at Drybrook in 1847 and was responsible for the chapel/schoolrooms at Woodside and Hoarthorns. He mentions the visits of John Wesley to Coleford in the mid-eighteenth century, the later work of congregationalists and the occasional visits of open-air preachers but does not consider the general rise of nonconformity in the Forest. He was moved by the poverty of the people, at one time barely able to provide clothes for the children to attend school, or to supply a slice of bread for their lunch.

Flaxley Abbey warranted a chapter of its own with references to the early charters and grants to the Cistercian foundation and to the humanitarian work in the local community of Catharine Boevy, friend of Addison and Steele. There is an extended footnote on the fine workmanship of the newly rebuilt Flaxley church. He notes that now that the furnace and forge have ceased, the Vale of Castiard is 'once more devoted wholly to the picturesque' and a return to the peaceable and quiet setting as granted to the monks by Henry II. He also refers to the healing properties of the iron-enriched waters of St Anthony's Well in that secluded spot in the beech woods below Edge Hill.

The Forest of Dean is not an easy read. It is crammed with statistics of production figures and prices, local place names not always easily identifiable, and dates of documents. But it is a unique and massive source of information. And Cyril Hart, who has written extensively on the Forest, says that the area 'would today have been poorer but for the efforts of this pioneer of local history. One must be grateful that, side by side with his important and exacting vocation, Nicholls made the time and acquired the energy to use his scholarship in seeking and recording for others the obscure story of the interesting Forest and neighbourhood in which he resided'.

So for Nicholls the landscape of the Forest was one of rapid industrial development providing employment for thousands of men and, although he was conscious of the beauty of its woodland, the Forest economy was more important to him. The extensive planting of conifers by the Forestry Commission only began in 1919 and the early nineteenth century planting of oak woodland had not reached maturity in his day, so industrial features and church buildings were much more conspicuous than they are today. The iron and coal mines, whose names figure so prominently in the book, have gone with few traces. Small inconspicuous fenced-off areas hidden among the trees with partially filled shafts in the case of coal mines and holes that disappear in the darkness underground in the case of the iron mines are all that remain.

Places to visit: Holy Trinity Church, Drybrook where he was vicar. Hope Well Free Mine where it is possible to go underground. Wimberry Slade and Bix Slade for coal mining remains and present day free mines. Darkhill, near Coleford for remains of iron works. Woods near Cannop Ponds for early nineteenth century oak plantings. Furnaces at Guns' Mill and Whitecliff. The Linear Park at Cinderford also displays information boards of old industrial sites and the communication lines associated with them.

J. Arthur Gibbs

The Landscapes of Country Sports around Bibury

A Cotswold Village, 1898

The first popular book to be published on the Cotswold landscape was *A Cotswold Village* by J. Arthur Gibbs. Gibbs was born in Westminster in 1867 and came from a Devon banking family. He was educated at Eton and Christ Church, Oxford, and after briefly sampling banking life in the city, moved to Ablington Manor, which his widowed mother began to rent in 1892 [fig. 28]. Here he lived as a young Victorian country gentleman, enjoying hunting, shooting, and fishing but also observing village life and its natural setting through the changing seasons. He was very well-read in the classics and English literature. He mixed easily with the local people as he had a sensitive and considerate manner. His book, which he said was written for amusement rather than for instruction, was published in 1898, a few months before his death at the early age of 31.

He began by distancing the Cotswolds from London, not only by a long train journey to Cirencester and then a weary seven mile walk and by the descriptions of the passing landscapes seen through the railway carriage windows, but also by the contrast between the noise and smoke, the dust and heat of the city, and the fresh green countryside. He found it an old-fashioned place. Villages, gardens, people and their clothes are all described as old-fashioned, not in the derogatory sense of out-moded, out of date and redundant but in the sense of genuine and unspoilt, 'each village familiar with forgotten years'. He conveys an image of a remote, untouched area, where he was glad to leave the coinage of the bank, for the gold of the sunshine and the silver of the trout stream.

The growing railway network had begun to change the countryside and Gibbs recognised the serious impact of the corresponding decline of stage-coach connections on those Cotswold towns not on the newly constructed lines. The nearest railway station to Northleach was Chedworth, and Bampton served Burford. Both stations were several miles away from these towns. Fairford too was isolated until a branch line from Oxford reached it in 1873. There were, however, seven trains a day each way between Cirencester and Paddington, and four trains each way from Foss Cross, the nearest station to Bibury, when the Midland and South Western Junction Line was opened in 1891. The effect of the

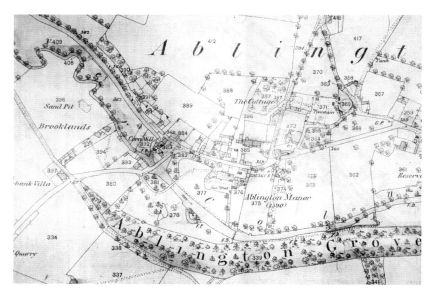

28. MAP OF
ABLINGTON
MANOR AT
THE TIME OF
J. ARTHUR
GIBBS

demise of coaching was repeated both in the early 1960s with the closure of these railway lines and in the 1970s with the reduction of the rural bus services, but these consequences were felt by different sections of the population.

Roads were sticky in the winter because they were still mended with limestone from roadside quarries. Cycle touring was just beginning. Cycling widened the range of places to visit to some thirty miles and Gibbs thought it would even increase the marketability of remote country houses. The motor car was not considered. Most travel was on foot, or by pony and trap, and he thought that there was little tourist potential in the Cotswolds. 'There is really nothing to see' he wrote. Ironically, his book was one of the first to stimulate that interest.

Local writers usually refer to the visible features of the landscape, to fields, woods and buildings, and to colours and forms. Gibbs more than most is aware of the sounds. Bird calls such as the caw of rooks, the clatter of the nightjar, the croak of the corncrake; the sounds of the river, the murmur of the water, the swish of the angler's rod, the splash of the trout; the sounds of the hunt, hounds crashing through the undergrowth and the huntsman's horn, are all reported. There was also the tinkling sheep bell, the hum of the threshing machine in the farmyard, and children's voices. There was no continuous background noise of road traffic, or the din of aircraft. He enjoyed the songs of the village feasts, as many as forty in an evening, often in Gloucestershire dialect. But he disapproved of the attempts, by organist or vicar, to substitute inferior modern hymns for the well-known traditional ones.

His landscape was a populated one. Farmers and farm labourers, keepers and poachers, carriers and hawkers, parsons and squires, millers and carters, were met and greeted. Gibbs thought that the gulf between the social classes was too great and did what he could to reduce it, but some of his comments are still patronising to today's ears. The rural population was declining, farm labourers were leaving their 12s. to 14s. a week employment and moving to find work in the cities and coal mines, or to join the army, or in some cases emigrating to the New World. He predicted that the villages of the Coln valley would be empty by the year 2000 if the trend continued for much longer. Possession of the 'elixir of life—pure air, fresh clear spring water, and sunshine', was insufficient to keep people in the area and Gibbs noted that, even before the agricultural depression with its stimulus to migration, many farm workers were used to moving house each year.

Irrespective of age, or size, or function, the village buildings harmonise. 'There is scarcely a building which is not in strict conformity or good taste', he wrote. He did not attribute this to the properties of the building stone, as Massingham did later, but to the integrity of the builders. These were generally 'unknown men whose life and labour, interests and aspirations, are unrecorded, but who have left us their adoration in their architecture'. Wayside crosses, tithe barns, bridges, manor houses and cottages [fig. 29], as well as magnificent churches, bear witness that 'they knew they worked under the eye of a great task master', so nothing offended and there was no forceful and jarring reminder of the utilitarian spirit of the late nineteenth century in the Cotswolds.

The poverty caused by the agricultural depression meant that building maintenance was often delayed, some houses were empty and properties were described as time worn. They were also, invariably, ivy clad, as contemporary photographs show. Today we find virginia creeper, wisteria, roses and vines, but rarely ivy on the walls of the houses. Gibbs recognised ivy's rapacious nature but not its damaging effects on mortar.

29. JOHN BROWN'S COTTAGE

The manor house at Ablington, built in 1590 by John Coxwell, had its gables and bell tower, lattice windows and oak beams—some of the latter came from Bibury church roof in 1863 and Gibbs mused on the human history witnessed by these timbers. But perhaps the most striking detail is that he was able on his first visit to walk unhindered into the unoccupied and unlocked house and to view its seventeenth century family portraits, antique oak furniture and collection of armour from the Civil War. No security systems or burglar alarms were required in those days.

He wrote at a time when it was difficult to sell or let farmland and he referred to fields that had once been cultivated but were now abandonned to grass or weeds, 'tumbled down' land. He thought it had not paid farmers to cultivate land since 1880 and that they were paying the wages of their labourers from their own capital. However, the light, calcareous soils of the Cotswolds were excellent for barley. This was the leading cereal and was sold for malting. Contemporary records show that barley from the Manor Farm went to local breweries in Cheltenham, Stroud and Cirencester and to more distant ones in Bristol and Reading. In 1895–6 barley prices surpassed those for wheat, so the Cotswolds were not as disadvantaged as some other areas in England. Wheat was sold to millers at Tewkesbury, Cirencester, Faringdon and Bibury. Oats were also important at the time because of the demand for horse feed, and when sold usually went to local farmers and millers.

The wetter bottoms and hollows and the more steeply sloping downs were under permanent pasture. Farms there were mixed, with sheep, dairy and store cattle besides the arable crops. Gibbs mentioned two notable Cotswold farmers, William Garne of Aldsworth, famous for his flock of prize-winning Cotswold sheep, and Hobbs of Maiseyhampton for

30. ABLINGTON DOWNS. THE ASYMMETRICAL DRY VALLEY WAS CUT BY PERIGLACIAL MELTWATER.
GIBBS OFTEN WALKED OR RODE HERE

his Oxford Down sheep, though apparently the cross-bred Cotswold/Hampshire Down animals were becoming more popular than either of these two pure breeds.

The constraints of wet valley bottoms and steep gradients of dry valley sides, some with turf rolls and scars indicating slope instability in saturated conditions [fig. 30], still apply today. So land use patterns are similar to those a hundred years ago. The dazzling yellow of oil seed rape has replaced acres of the pink carnation colour of sainfoin and set-aside is perhaps marginally preferable to tumbled down land, but otherwise Gibbs' wish for more prosperous farming could be repeated at the beginning of the twenty-first century.

He was well aware of the difference between valley and wold. Valleys were sheltered, green and vibrant; wolds were bleak, grey and dull. Valleys were intimate, well wooded and homely; wolds were expansive, sparsely populated and chill. Yet he was not entirely consistent because the bracing, invigorating air of the wolds was an attractive feature of the whole area for him and the rural economy and field sports depended on linking both together.

Gibbs enjoyed traditional country sports, particularly fox hunting and trout fishing and wrote about them with enthusiasm and knowledge. To ride at high speed with the hounds over the wolds in the company of skilled horsemen and women was for him an exhilarating experience. He analysed the conditions that made for a good run. The fox should be fit and wise, having learnt as a cub to leave the covert as soon as the hounds arrive. The 'old customer' living in the Manor grounds was such a one. Dry leaves, turbulent air, and clinging soil reduced the scent left by a fox, so ideal conditions for a 'burning scent' were anticyclonic, with a light N.E. wind, an early morning dew, rough grass, and an air temperature between 3 and 8 degrees Celsius. The scent increases as the animal warms and declines as it tires, ceasing altogether after about 20 minutes.

Fox coverts of three to four acres are still conspicuous features of the Cotswold landscape, 'sacred institutions', Gibbs called them. They are fenced off woodlands, with no access paths, where the fox earths are safe. They are not normally old woods and often contain conifers such as spruce. They are managed for their dense undergrowth. Their spacing determines the length of runs and significantly, when in the early twentieth century much farmland was sold or let by the old land-owning families, the fox coverts were retained.

With much tumbled down land and pasture and low stone walls, sometimes with jumps, riding was relatively easy. Ridge and furrow, boggy ground, deeply ploughed 'pewy' fields and barbed wire, were rare hazards on the Cotswolds, although it was suggested that hares sometimes diverted the attention of immature hounds.

The hunting season lasted from September to May, and Ablington was in the territory of the Vale of the White Horse Hunt. Meets were held at both Ablington Manor and Bibury Court [fig. 31]. The hounds were kept at Cirencester Park and Gibbs said there were more than two hundred hunters stabled in Cirencester. Ancillary events were the annual Hunt Ball, horse shows at Lechlade and Cirencester and point to point races at Andoversford, Moreton-in-Marsh, Oaksey and Sherston.

Not all farmers welcomed the hunt and damage occurred to crops as well as to gates and fences, but loss of poultry to foxes was of greater concern and Gibbs commented that,

31. BIBURY COURT FROM THE COLN ST.ALDWYNS ROAD, A VIEW THAT GIBBS THOUGHT IT WORTH
WALKING MILES TO SEE

with the severity of the agricultural depression, hunting was the principal factor in money circulation in the countryside at the time.

Shooting brought food for all sections of the rural population in winter months. On some of the larger estates, such as Sherborne, Barnsley and Stowell, pheasants were reared but on most of the estates the birds were wild. Partridges were shot at the end of harvest when they were less timid and some farmers used a hawk kite to keep the partridges from flying off before the guns were near. Pigeon shooting was also popular with the farmers. Snipe arrived at the withy beds and water meadows in November and wild fowl—mallard, teal and wigeon—were available along the Coln all through the winter. Hares and rabbits were plentiful and most bags included birds no longer found in the area—quail, corncrake, golden plover and woodcock. Gibbs recognised the contribution of shooting to the decline of the bird population. Shooting the occasional heron was acceptable because of the damage it could cause to trout stocks, but not the peregrine falcon.

The Coln, which is still a trout river, flows through the grounds of Ablington Manor. From Stowell Park to Lechlade fifteen miles of fishing rights were held by the principal land owners and by the two fishing inns, the Bull at Fairford and the Swan at Bibury. The river was managed for trout fishing [fig. 32]. Trout grow best in water that is cool and deep, with high oxygen and calcium carbonate content. Frequent springs along its bed maintain the water levels and the calcium carbonate content and also regulate the temperature. Management can also help by providing trees to shade the water, by adding stones, fir poles and artificial waterfalls to increase the turbulence of the water and thus the oxygen content and by digging holes in the river bed to provide deeper water where the current slows and the fish use less energy in swimming. At Ablington the river had been widened and an island formed, although this has now disappeared. Gibbs thought that the marshy areas along the valley could be modified for fish. The trout farm at Bibury came a few years later in 1906.

Food for trout was varied and abundant. Flies, caddis larvae and small snails were provided. Flies were preferred by the fish, so fishing was by artificial fly, varied according to the season. Gibbs mentions some of the flies—March Brown, Blue, Yellow and Olive Dun in April, Green Drake in June and Red Palmer in July.

Some fresh stock from Loch Leven was introduced from time to time but most were indigenous fish. Their size increased down stream from an average 1lb at Bibury, to 3lbs in the Broad Water of Fairford Park. Predators were otters, pike and herons, but many years of good fishing were recorded. Normally rods could be spaced at two-thirds of a mile intervals, except in early June when the mayfly were hatching and the river 'boiled'. Then they could be as close as 100 yards. Gibbs was a keen angler and the river provided him with quiet, homely scenes all the year round.

His major sporting interest, however, was cricket. He had played for Somerset and the M.C.C. and also enjoyed the less predictable village fixtures at Winson. He thought that farm labourers were generally too tired to commit themselves to cricket matches in their leisure time but there was strong interest among the farmers. The shallow, stony soil of the Cotswolds and the lack of suitable flat land near the villages were handicaps for cricket but there were good and successful clubs at Bourton, Northleach and Cirencester. He advised on a mixed clay and water top dressing and frequent rolling to prepare better wickets. For the development of character, coolness and courage, hunting and cricket were, in his opinion, superior to cycling and golf!

32. TROUT FISHING ON
THE COLN AT BIBURY

The name of Bibury was also associated with horse racing. On Barrington Downs, near Aldsworth, was the old Bibury racecourse. Its grandstand is marked on Isaac Taylor's map of 1777 and records of racing there go back to 1681. The springy turf and the wide open spaces were ideal for horses and the course was a significant feature of the Sherborne estate. The racing was patronised by royalty, and inevitably attracted social accolites. Macaroni Farm preserves in its name the memory of young dandies.

Gibbs was a competent naturalist and took a great delight in the wild flowers of the Cotswolds. He wrote of their forms and colours, and noted the prevalence of golden yellow. Gold was the Cotswold colour. He distinguished between the flowers along the banks of the Coln, those of the grassy downs, those of the hedgerows and dusty road side verges and those of the arable fields. Only charlock in the barley fields is missing today from the species he lists but the numbers are greatly reduced. He was the first of several writers to refer to the richness and variety of flowers to be found in the clearings of the old oak woodlands at Chedworth, where the soil contains more clay, and was probably one of the last to comment seriously on the herbal remedies advocated by the village quack.

Nearly sixty species of bird are mentioned, mainly larger varieties, although the yellow hammer was described as the 'herald of Bibury'. There were enormous flocks of golden plover, and such rarities as marsh harriers, grey phalarope and long- and short-eared owls could be seen. No corncrakes were recorded in 1897 and woodpeckers were uncommon, but there were shrikes, nightjars, and wimbrels. Kingfishers were often seen. He noted that here, as in England generally, the bird population was in decline.

Just as his views on architecture were influenced by John Ruskin and on fishing by Isaac Walton, so his writing on natural history owed much to Richard Jeffries, who provided a model for him. Gibbs style of writing is comfortable and gentle, and unedited versions of his book are punctuated by quotations from classical authors, especially Horace, and from the English poets. Gray's elegy strongly influenced his perception of the countryside and so did his Christian belief. Thus he concludes his book, as he recalled walking over Ablington Downs on a summer evening, with these words, 'I cannot but believe that there arise from the secret parts of this beautiful earth, at dawn of day and at eventide, other voices beside the ineffable songs of birds, the rustling murmurs that whisper in the woods, and the plaintive babbling of the brooks, hymns of unknown depths of harmony, impossible to describe, because impossible to imagine, crying night and day, "Blessing and honour and glory and power be unto Him that sitteth upon the throne …".'

Gibbs clearly enjoyed living in the Cotswolds and found much in village life and in the natural world to interest him. One senses that as he looked at the woods, fields and rivers he took pleasure in them as they were but also reflected on their potential for the fox, partridge and trout.

Places to visit: Ablington for manor, mill, farm and barns. Ablington Downs for flora and periglacial landforms. Bibury for church, trout fishing and Bibury Court.

H.A. EVANS

GUIDING THE EDWARDIAN TOURIST THROUGH THE COTSWOLDS

Oxford and the Cotswolds, 1905

Just before Christmas 1905 Macmillan published *Oxford and the Cotswolds* in their *Highways and Byways* series. It was written for the Edwardian tourist by Herbert A. Evans and illustrated with engravings by F.L. Griggs. Evans had been an undergraduate at Balliol College, Oxford and then a schoolmaster and private tutor and, although he refers to the Cotswolds in other seasons, the book is essentially a guide for a cycle tour in the long summer vacation. Norman Jewson brought a copy of the book with him when he first visited the area in the summer of 1907. Although it covers a larger area, it is with the Cotswolds that the present chapter is concerned.

There were few cars on the roads in those days and Evans had reservations about the ability of cars to cope with some of the steep gradients, as for example at Fossbridge and Caudle Green [fig. 33], and anyway thought the car inappropriate for exploring the intimate landscape of the Cotswolds. The bicycle gave more freedom of movement and at ten miles per hour (the same speed as the stage-coach) sufficient distances could be covered in a day to satisfy the wayfarer. There were also good opportunities for walks along the river valleys such as the Eye at the Slaughters, the Windrush from Bourton-on-the-Water to Ford, the Evenlode at Oddington and the Holy Brook at Tunley. Another recommended walk was along the foot of the escarpment from Broadway to Sudeley. It was then usually possible to walk freely on private land.

By 1905 the main roads had been surfaced with Clee Hill roadstone and Leicester grit but most of the gated side roads were of local Oolite, dusty when dry and sticky when wet. The roadside pits from which the stone had been dug were still treacherous.

Evans made a series of day excursions from strategically placed inns. These included the Talbot at Stow, the Lygon Arms at Broadway, the White Hart at Winchcombe and the Fossbridge. He stopped for lunch at others and was partial to a glass of cider, but few Cotswold inns could supply his wants in this respect, for cider was not a Cotswold product. So he compliments the Golden Ball at Lower Swell, the Plough at Ford and the Fox at Little Barrington for doing so.

33. CAUDLE
GREEN. EVANS
THOUGHT THE
HILLS WERE
TOO STEEP
FOR CARS

He recognised the genuine Cotswold landscape as he approached from the east over the Evenlode valley at Adlestrop. The rolling upland, still with traces of its ancient sheep walks, the winding valleys with their rich water meadows and clear trout streams, the grey stone villages with their churches and manors, the weather-beaten ash trees along the dry stone walls of the field boundaries and the oak and hazel fox coverts were noted as making the peculiar genius of the Cotswolds. The market towns he visited were each described with his immediate reaction: Painswick—clean, trim, with a modern air; Chipping Campden—the most distinctive and expressive town of the area, reserved, uneccentric, sedate, outwardly unchanged for three hundred years; Northleach—desolate, decayed and forlorn, with grass growing in the streets; Cirencester—placid and dignified; and Burford—exclusive, select and aristocratic. Similarly some of the villages are succinctly portrayed: Condicote with a bleak and poverty-stricken air; Lower Slaughter, spruce with a wealthy and generous squire; Bledington, deserted and melancholy. The depressed state of agriculture had contributed to rural poverty and depopulation and Evans refers to the situation at Guiting Power in 1902 with thirty empty cottages and a population that had recently halved. Some of the fine old Cotswold manor houses were then unoccupied.

A major feature of the book is the descriptions of the churches. Evans methodically visited them and he emphasises their importance. The great wool churches are given extended treatment—Cirencester with its delicately carved three-story porch, Northleach [fig. 34] with its fluted nave pillars and wool merchants' brasses, Fairford with its unique set of medieval stained glass windows, Chipping Campden with its fine exterior expressing unity, magnificence and strength and Winchcombe with its abbey relics. Wool wealth was greatest in the fifteenth century, prices peaked in the 1480s, and the finely carved stonework of this period is seen to best advantage in these churches. A number of village churches also have Perpendicular features of the late fifteenth century, such as Chedworth which bears the date 1485 on its south wall and which Griggs illustrated.

34. PORCH
OF CHURCH
OF ST PETER
AND ST PAUL,
NORTHLEACH

There are about sixty Norman churches on the Cotswolds. The simplest architectural form has chancel, nave and south porch. Where there has not been a significant increase in population, or a wealthy endowment, these churches remain largely unaltered as at Upper Swell and Condicote. Where population growth has occurred aisles have been added, as at Bibury and Daglingworth, or a new nave built, as at Oddington and Lower Swell. A few Norman churches have beakhead ornamentation to their doorways and Evans mentions Windrush, Elkstone and the displaced doorway in a cottage at Sherborne in this respect. In some churches the chancel arch is decorated. Reference is also made to the sculptured tympana at Quenington and Elkstone. Some churches were originally built to a cruciform plan as Sevenhampton and Dowdeswell and others had transepts added at a later date as Guiting Power. Towers were added in the thirteenth century at Oddington but more

35. ST MICHAEL'S
CHURCH,
DUNTISBOURNE
ROUS

often in the fifteenth century, with broach spires at Dowdeswell and Aldsworth and a saddle back tower at Duntisbourne Rous [fig. 35]. The massive corner stones—the longs and shorts—of Saxon churches, the grotesques at Aldsworth, the gargoyles and corbel table at Elkstone and the Saxon sculptures at Daglingworth also attracted his attention. Typically he disapproved of the interior restoration work at Temple Guiting, Chipping Campden and Coberley and the poor quality deal seating at Little Barrington, but where fine oak pews, or seventeenth-century panelling, or Jacobean pulpits occur, as at Bledington, Buckland and Duntisbourne Rous respectively, they are praised.

Evans was also attracted by some of the church memorials—the tablets, monuments and effigies of members of historic families, such as the Pooles and Atkyns at Sapperton and the Hicks at Chipping Campden and of individuals such as Sir John Blaket at Icomb, Sir John Fortesque at Ebrington and Dr George Talbot at Temple Guiting. Strangely he omits the Dutton monuments at Sherborne. Collections of bale top tombs and brass memorial plates are noted and he reminds his readers that churchyards were at one time fashionable places in which to walk.

The descriptions of the churches are enhanced by the engravings of F.L. Griggs [fig. 36]. Griggs was thought to be the finest architectural draughtsman of his day and his illustrations

36. GRIGG'S ENGRAVING OF THE PORCH AT
NORTHLEACH (1905)

for this book, which was one of ten in the *Highways and Byways* series he worked on, are of particularly high quality. So much so that Macmillan complained at their slow rate of production suggesting that, as readers do not spend half an hour looking at each picture, he put too much labour into them. In fact he only managed to complete seventy-two of the projected eighty illustrations and was paid accordingly!

In 1903 Griggs moved from his home town of Hitchin specifically for this work and settled in Chipping Campden, where he stayed for the rest of his life. Some of the scenes of his illustrations were revisited for later engravings, often for special purposes. So for example an engraving of the tiny Saxon church at Duntisbourne Rous [fig. 37], with sheep grazing on the lower slopes in the evening light, was dedicated to the memory of Ernest Gimson, who was married there. And the hidden Norman church at Stanley Pontlarge was drawn for a wedding gift. It has been suggested that Griggs' engravings have a hint of pilgrimage in them. In these relatively early works, and he said it took at least forty years to learn to draw properly, there was already that characteristic handling of light, sunlight absorbed by some parts of a building and reflected from others and those small figures of people which gave scale and human access to the picture, that distinguished his later work.

In addition to churches, Griggs illustrated landscape views, manor houses such as the porches of Upper Swell and Upper Slaughter manors, and groups of buildings along streets such as Gloucester Street in Winchcombe and Vicarage Lane in Painswick.

Some of the manor houses were visited and described by Evans, especially if there was a story about a

37. GRIGG'S ENGRAVING OF ST.MICHAEL'S [1904]

previous occupant. He seems to have gained access to them by referring to the *Highways and Byways* series and to his projected contribution to it. There are numerous references to the Civil War and to the movement of troops across the Cotswolds. He mentions the mansion at Chipping Campden which was built in 1613 for Sir Baptist Hicks at a cost of £29,000 and used as a Royalist garrison and then burnt down so that the enemy could not take it. Sudeley Castle was also left as a Civil War ruin. Charles I held court at Painswick, hence the name of Court House. With reference to country houses Evans, like Massingham, preferred the Jacobean Bibury Court to the Italianate style of Sherborne, Rendcomb and Sandywell. He noted that many Tudor manors had been demolished, as for example at Sapperton, and others had been demoted to tenant farm houses as at Upper Swell, Upper Slaughter and Cassey Compton.

He was also interested in links between the Cotswolds and Oxford University. So he thought that the manor farm at Temple Guiting [fig. 38] would make an ideal vacation retreat for the President and Fellows of Corpus Christi College, for here the college still owns most of the land. The hillside church at Saintbury was mentioned for its former rector William Latimer, who helped to re-establish the teaching of Greek at Oxford. The earthwork remains of Brimpsfield castle were associated with John Gifford, the founder of Worcester College (formerly Gloucester College), where Benedictines such as Richard Kyderminster,

38. MANOR FARM AT
TEMPLE GUITING

abbot of Winchcombe, were educated. The Keble and Wadham connections with Eastleach
and Southrop were not explored.

Cycling at a leisurely pace brought him to view points where he could rest and appreciate
the scenery. Thus he stopped at several sites along the crest of the escarpment, such as
Dover's Hill, Broadway Tower, Birdlip and Painswick Beacon, where the panorama is
far-reaching. Other views were more circumscribed and intimate as the Golden Valley
from Sapperton church, or the Isbourne Valley from Langley Hill. He was also able to
observe the fields he passed with wheat, barley and oats approaching harvest and the
cheerful brilliant pink fields of sainfoin—a native plant cultivated on the Cotswolds since
the mid-seventeenth century. The lush cattle pastures along the Coln below Stowell Park
remain as Evans described them, but fat lambs have displaced mutton as the main product
of sheep farming, just as mutton from the crossbred Cotswold/Hampshire Downs flocks
had displaced the wool production of the pure bred Cotswold. Teams of oxen could still
be seen ploughing in a few locations.

There were large areas of furze and heath and many small plantations of conifers. Relics
of the open field system remained at Westcott, with grass baulks between the cultivated
strips, but elsewhere it was an enclosed landscape of dry stone walls and hedges. Evans
said that enclosure on the Cotswolds and the new farming system associated with it began
with Lord Bathurst at Cirencester and commented on the leading role of Cirencester in
agricultural development with its important market for corn and sheep and its Royal
Agricultural College.

Cirencester was also the hunting centre. Both winter visitors and local residents could
ride with the hounds from Monday to Saturday and Evans gives the territories of the
various Cotswold hunts. But here, and for country sports generally, he defers to Gibbs
for first-hand knowledge. Rendcomb and Temple Guiting were noted as excellent riding
areas. The famous trout rivers, the Coln and Windrush, were well known to Oxford
undergraduates as were Bibury races to earlier generations of students. Few traces of the
old race course on Barrington Downs remained but the Coln could still be fished at

Fairford for a 2s. 6p. (12p.) ticket. The traditional Cotswold games on Dover's Hill, which had to be stopped in 1851, bowls on the green at the Falcon in Painswick and cricket at Bourton-on-the-Water were included in his other references to sport.

A cycle tour gave access to the habitats of the rarer flowers—to Langley Hill for the greater burnet saxifrage (*Pimpinella major*), to Painswick Woods and Beacon for the red helleborine (*Cephalanthera rubra*), which he would have been very fortunate to have seen, and several different species of orchid, to Chedworth Wood for lily of the valley. But generally the speed of travel along the lanes meant reference was made to the main colonies of plants, to willow herb, wild angelica and travellers' joy, depending on the season, rather than to individual flowers. Walks along the Windrush and its tributaries brought him to patches of mimulus and along the Evenlode to marsh marigolds. The floral references indicate that Evans had knowledge of the area at other times of the year as well as during the summer vacation.

Cycling is a quiet form of transport so there are surprisingly few comments on other wildlife. Amongst birds he mentions blackcap, whinchat and turtle-dove, while for animals it was necessary to sit and wait for the stoat and water vole and, apart from blues and burnets, butterflies are not recorded, although in his book on Gloucestershire published in 1925, he wrote that more than half of all British species were to be found in the county.

Evans was well-read and had consulted the two major early histories of the county: Atkyns' *Ancient and Present State of Gloucestershire* (1712) and Rudder's *History of Gloucestershire* (1779). He quoted Macaulay's *History of England* for broader historical perspectives and Anthony Wood's *Athenæ Oxonienses* for the Oxford references. He used published histories of towns, churches and archaeological sites and the recently written *A Cotswold Village* by J. Arthur Gibbs. He appreciated the collection of books available to the visitor staying at the Plough at Ford and commented on the great library of Sir Thomas Phillips as he passed his former home, Middle Hill, above Broadway. Whenever he knew of a literary work connected to a Cotswold manor or town it is mentioned. Thus he explained the influence of Alexander Pope on the eighteenth century landscaping of Cirencester Park, with its five mile avenue, its glades and follies, laid out on formerly open uncultivated downland, and also the first attempts at landscape gardening of William Shenstone at Mickleton.

Some sites of ancient monuments were visited and their stories told, such as the gamekeeper's discovery of the Roman villa at Chedworth, the destruction of the splendour of the abbeys at Hailes and Winchcombe by Thomas, Lord Seymour and the Roman finds at Cirencester. But others are missed, such as the long barrow of Belas Knap, and no mention is made of the many deserted villages he must have passed or even walked over.

The great medieval wool collecting centres of Northleach and Chipping Campden, with their wool warehouses, merchants' homes and packhorse routes linking them locally with the sheep walks and distantly with the ports for exporting to Flanders, are well treated. There are only hints of that other period of wool prosperity in the eighteenth and early nineteenth centuries in the Stroud area and barely a mention of the woollen mills spread along the Frome valley that Evans travelled. His cycle tour did not extend further south than this.

One of his informants was C.R. Ashbee, the leader of the Guild of Handicraft, who had bought the old silk mill in Chipping Campden in 1902. The Guild consisted of a group of distinguished craftsmen—metalworkers, woodcarvers, bookbinders and jewellers—who moved from east London. Ashbee himself began the work of restoring the vernacular architecture of the area. He was strongly influenced by William Morris, as were Ernest Gimson and the Barnsley brothers at Sapperton, and Evans commended the beautiful, useful and durable furniture produced at Sapperton and displayed in the showrooms at Daneway House.

The Arts and Crafts movement had influenced Evans' appreciation of Cotswold buildings and he recognised the unsuitability of red bricks and red tiles as building materials for the area and of Welsh slate as a roofing material, as used for example on the Bull at Fairford. He was apprehensive about the impact of the railways, which although they gave passengers delightful scenic views, also brought red-brick buildings around the stations, telegraph poles along the lines and signal boxes and other obtrusive features. He expressed foreboding over the possible effect on Buckland, Stanton and Stanway of the Cheltenham-Stratford line, which was due to open in 1906.

His descriptions of September mists along the valley floors, October frosts and autumnal tints, the healthy bracing wind of the Cotswold edge and the keen invigorating air at Stow, attract the visitor but these are balanced by reference to the bleakness of the high windswept villages and to the snow drifts that incredibly, at Brockhampton, lasted till August in 1634.

The book is a discursive, anecdotal and leisurely guide and was welcomed by a whole generation of visitors to the Cotswolds. Evans wrote with these tourists in mind, drawing attention to the features of the landscape he thought would interest them and conforming to the overall policy of the *Highways and Byways* series. As a guide it is still useful today. It was one of a number taking a similar approach, being preceded by W.H. Hutton's *By Thames and Cotswold* in 1903 and followed years later by R.P. Beckinsale's *Companion into Gloucestershire and the Cotswolds* in 1948 and more recently by C.W.J. Withers' *Discovering the Cotswolds* in 1990.

Places to visit: Chipping Campden for church, almshouses, silk mill and F.L. Griggs connections; Winchcombe for church, former George Hotel with its abbey connection, White Hart where Evans stayed and Sudeley Castle; Duntisbourne Rous for church and setting; Upper and Lower Swell for churches and manor.

Norman Jewson

Exposure to the Attitudes of the Sapperton Craftsmen

By Chance I did Rove, 1951

Norman Jewson was born in Norwich in 1884 into the well-known family of timber merchants. After graduating from Cambridge and a period working as an architectural apprentice in London, he came on a sketching holiday to the Cotswolds in the summer of 1907. The Cotswolds were then a little-known area, he said, where old customs and traditional ways of life lingered on. Like Arthur Gibbs he arrived by train at Cirencester station. He brought with him Evan's *Highways and Byways of Oxford and the Cotswolds* and guided by this, and the whim of a hired donkey, spent several weeks drawing those architectural features of the area that attracted his interest. Griggs' engravings and Evans' descriptions led him to such delights as the cross at Calmsden, the manor houses at Upper Swell and Upper Slaughter, the porches of Northleach and Cirencester churches and to the remote setting of Cassey Compton. Apart from a stay at the former Swan Inn in Chipping Campden this was a camping holiday. Then, before catching the train back to London he made a visit to Sapperton. He felt his excuses for arriving unannounced at Ernest Gimson's house were flimsy, but was immediately welcomed, and within a few hours of viewing the display of Gimson's furniture at Daneway and talking to the great man himself he had accepted the kindly offer of a month's experience as an 'improver'. Jewson remained at Sapperton for the rest of his life, another sixty-eight years! In 1951 he published a little book of reminiscences of his time here in the years before and during the First World War. This charming book *By Chance I Did Rove* is especially important for its insight into the Arts and Crafts movement in the Cotswolds. In this chapter we shall comment on some of the themes of Jewson's book, but will first look at its setting.

Sapperton village is situated above the steep-sided valley of the Frome but just below the exposed plateau, its main street following a gently sweeping curve on the south-east side of the valley. All the main Cotswold rivers have valleys which are aligned in alternating north–south and north-west–south-east sections. This alignment is unusual as neither geological faulting nor the joint pattern of the rocks explain it. The Frome typically follows this north–south direction from its source at Brimpsfield, but then at Sapperton, instead of turning south-eastwards as the land surface suggests it once did through a wind gap towards Thames Head, it veers sharply westwards, having been captured by a vigorously eroding stream flowing into the Severn. The steeper gradient to the Severn and the large volume of spring water, especially from its north bank tributaries, have enabled the deep incision of the Frome to form what is known as the Golden Valley.

The valley sides are often stepped. These steps reflect the geological structure but earlier agriculture may have contributed to the relatively flat pastureland separated by steeper wooded banks north of the village. In fact the Leasowes here were formerly cultivated strips of common land. There has been some slumping along the valley sides and what is possibly a large rotational slide has occurred at Daneway Bank. The brashy soil of the surrounding plateau is derived from the Great Oolite, but Fuller's Earth outcrops on the valley sides and this explains the succession of springs on both sides of the valley. St Kenelm's spring near the church formerly supplied the village with its water.

The Frome valley is well wooded and the woodland here is predominantly of beech with some oak and ash and a hazel understorey. Some of the beech trees on the Bathurst estate were planted and some are from natural regeneration. There are several rapidly decaying old specimen trees in Sapperton Park and others were planted on the tumps formed of waste from the digging of the tunnel for the Severn–Thames Canal. With regard to furniture-making, in the Cotswolds beech was not used much, but at Daneway sawmills Job Gardiner produced plane blocks and brush backs of beech. The dense shade and deep leaf litter in the woods restrict the ground flora, but bluebells thrive in the spring and the beech trees make a significant visual contribution to the valley in all seasons.

There are some scattered oaks and one large old tree Jewson mentions is by the lane to Sapperton mill. Local oak was the main type of wood used in building construction and in furniture-making. Walnut was also used in furniture-making and walnut trees were found in Ernest Barnsley's garden, one still stands, and in an avenue at King's Farm, Tunley.

39. LILY OF THE VALLEY GROWING IN SICCARIDGE WOOD

Most Cotswold beech woods contain yew trees and at Pinbury Park is a famous yew avenue dating from the Middle Ages and known as Nuns' Walk. Another group, some native, some Italian, borders the path through the churchyard and beneath these trees are the graves of Gimson and the Barnsleys. A feature of many gardens in the village is yew topiary with shapes of cones, houses, birds and cheeses. Recently a line of yews has been planted along the approach road to Sapperton on land known as the Butts, where archery practice once took place. The wych elms Jewson mentions have all gone as a result of the ravages of Dutch elm disease.

The ground flora of the woods at Sapperton vary with the shade, drainage and soil type. Jewson mentions the lily of the valley [fig. 39], which still flourishes on the limestone scree slopes of Siccaridge Wood, and Solomon's seal over the entrance to the canal tunnel. He also refers to green hellebore, herb paris, spurge laurel, bird's nest orchid and deadly nightshade—all typical limestone woodland plants.

Daneway Bank has a rich grassland flora and the hedgerows of the lanes descending to the Frome and its tributary streams are colourful throughout spring and summer. Jewson notes violet, bloody cranesbill and wood sorrel in Tunley Lane and the special visits to Battlescombe for wild daffodils and further away to Oaksey for fritillaries and to Barnsley for pasque flowers. As with several other of our writers he distinguishes between the flowers of wood, meadow and hedgerow, but he also notices the flowers of the dry stone walls—pennywort, toadflax, stonecrop and pellitory of the wall.

He enjoyed his evening walks with Ernest Gimson, who was a careful observer of nature. Gimson encouraged him to draw a different wild flower each day and to concentrate on the simplified characteristics of the flower which could then form the basic design pattern for plasterwork, woodcarving, or needlework. A museum piece example of this at Cheltenham is a brass candle sconce incorporating a pattern of snakes head fritillaries [fig. 40].

Jewson's book is one of the principal sources of information on the Arts and Crafts movement in the Cotswolds and he tells how Sapperton had become a centre for the

40. A FIELD OF
SNAKE'S HEAD
FRITILLARIES

movement at the end of the nineteenth century. Three young architect friends Ernest Gimson, Ernest Barnsley and Sidney Barnsley had arrived in the Cotswolds in 1893. They thought that architecture and craftwork were interdependent and, as they found they could not settle to pursue their ideals in an urban practice, they sought a rural setting. They chose the Cotswolds partly because of William Morris' influence—Morris came to Kelmscott in 1871 and his ideas inspired them—and partly because, although it was accessible to London and via the Fosse Way to Leicester, Gimson's home, it was an area relatively untouched by commercialism, industrialisation and mass production, and where there was still a respect for quality workmanship and a reservoir of skilled craftsmen to be tapped. The friends were of independent means but here they also benefitted from the support of a wealthy, conservative landowner. Gimson's plan was to eventually set up a colony of craftsmen and, by drawing inspiration from nature, to produce buildings and furniture that were genuine and honest, and in which the materials, design and workmanship were in harmony. So for example, he considered that the design and modelling of plasterwork should be appropriate to the properties of the material. His representations of flowers and fruit, foliage and fauna, were simple, soft and flowing, often using the fourth finger to shape the plaster because of its more delicate touch and he drew on the traditional techniques of previous centuries to which his later showrooms at Daneway House gave a constant reminder.

The isolated sixteenth century house at Pinbury [fig. 41] was discovered by Sidney Barnsley on a walk. Like many similar properties it was in a delapidated state at the time and was taken on a repairing lease from the Bathursts, who had previously let it as a

41. VIEW OF PINBURY PARK. THE HOUSE AND OUTBUILDINGS WERE LEASED TO GIMSON AND THE BARNSLEYS IN 1894

42. WORKSHOP AT PINBURY (1895). NOTICE THE CHEST, CHAIRS AND PLASTER PANELS
(CHELTENHAM MUSEUM)

farmhouse, having acquired it from Sir Robert Atkyns in the eighteenth century. The house was repaired, some outbuildings were converted to cottages and others to a workshop [fig. 42], and for the next seven years it was their base. The restoration of the property was of such quality, however, that Lord Bathurst wished to take it back and offered most generous terms. These were, that the three architects could select sites on his estate for new houses, which they could build to their own designs, at the estate's expense, and the combined rent for these three houses would be the same as that originally agreed for Pinbury i.e. £75 per annum. So in 1902–3 on land behind the church 'The Leasowes' was built by Ernest Gimson, 'Beech Hanger' by Sidney Barnsley, and 'Upper Dorvel House' [fig. 43] by Ernest Barnsley. The latter can be viewed from the north of the church, or from the lane to Sapperton mill. It consists of a pair of old cottages, possibly those shown in the Kip engraving of Sapperton Manor, to which wings have been added at each end. The north wing was inspired by the high tower at Daneway House. Local stone was used for the new wings, rubble from Sapperton quarry for the walls and dressed stone from Minchinhampton for the lintels and quoins. The other two houses are less easily seen.

Most of the cottages at Sapperton were traditionally built, where the landlord provided both the site and the materials, and the tenant the labour. Agricultural workers were expected to have a range of skills, one of which was drystone walling. So building the walls of a house was a straightforward task, especially when assistance with the main structural features such as chimneys, corners and doorways was available from the

43. UPPER DORVEL HOUSE, (HOME OF ERNEST BARNSLEY 1903–1926)

stone masons employed on the estate. Stone from the quarries in Sapperton parish was unsuitable for mullion windows or for lintels, so oak timber was normally used, although for more well-to-do tenants stone could be brought in. Roof slates came from Freeman's quarry at Througham Fields. The mortar preferred for buttered joints, i.e. joints flush with the surface, was made from lime and road drift. The size of a cottage reflected the circumstances of the tenant, so the wheelwright's or the saw-miller's houses were larger. Houses of the sixteenth to nineteenth centuries have strong similarities. Gimson and the Barnsleys recognised this and their own houses of the early twentieth century are in keeping with these earlier properties. They used local materials and local traditions of working, but did not slavishly copy the details of earlier periods. And there are several clearly visible architectural features that distinguish their work as an observation of Sapperton village hall or of Rodmarton Manor would show.

Horse-drawn transport had restricted the distance building materials could be conveniently carried for most houses, but the railways introduced Welsh slate for roofs and lorries brought cheap bricks and manufactured materials such as corrugated iron and concrete tiles. Also after the First World War there were fewer local craftsmen around so most Cotswold villages, including Sapperton, have some traces of this transitional phase before modern building regulations, requiring more appropriate materials, were imposed. Apart from a small council housing estate built in 1966 on former glebe land, and some very recent building, there have been few significant changes to the fabric of the village since the period Jewson describes.

He refers to the nineteenth-century farmhouses, Court Farm, Beacon Farm and Hailey Farm, farms whose layout corresponded to the piecemeal enclosure of the parish. He makes more extended comment on several historic properties such as Daneway and Pinbury. Daneway House had been a manor house in the fourteenth century, with a great hall and central fire with louvres in the roof to allow smoke to escape. The Hancox family were tenants from 1397 and later purchased the property. As the family progressed from yeomen to gentlemen so the house was modified. A major addition was the five storey tower wing of the seventeenth century. The house was bought by the Bathursts at the end of the nineteenth century and repaired by Ernest Barnsley. The rooms at Daneway then became showrooms for Gimson's furniture. The outbuildings were modified as workshops, and from 1907 till soon after Gimson's death in 1919, Daneway became the furniture-making centre.

In furniture-making all work was by hand and up to twelve men and local apprentices were employed. While Ernest Barnsley concentrated on architecture, Sidney Barnsley and Ernest Gimson, although they too had trained as architects and not as furniture designers and makers, found that their interest in furniture gradually took over. Skills were learned from other craftsmen such as chair-making from Philip Clissett, a bodger from Boseley near Ledbury, chamfering from the Sapperton wheelwright Richard Harrison, and others from the cabinet-makers they employed. Some ideas were derived from the careful observations they had made of Byzantine inlaid furniture and of farm implements, such as hay rakes and wagons. They aimed to produce furniture for everyday use, at reasonable costs such as £5 for an oak chest, but the hours of labour involved prevented this target from being reached. Jewson mentions 453 hours work and 47 hours supervision in making a sideboard!

Many manor houses or houses of manorial families, well built in the sixteenth and seventeenth centuries, were now in poor condition and had become tenant farm houses,

44. OWLPEN MANOR WHICH JEWSON BOUGHT TO RESTORE IN 1926

or were unoccupied. Jewson's walks in the surrounding countryside took him past some of these properties which in later years he would repair. He makes special reference to the sequence of fine houses along the Holy Brook valley from Rookswood to Wishanger. He repaired Througham, Througham Slad and Sydenhams in the 1930s. No doubt his favourite was Owlpen Manor [fig. 44], which he bought to restore in 1926. He modified Iles Farm at Far Oakridge in 1914 by joining a house to a barn. For the classic work of Ernest Barnsley at Rodmarton Manor, which began in 1906 and continued to 1926, Jewson finished the chapel in 1929. His own house in Sapperton was Batchelor's Court, which was formed between 1910 and 1915 by joining together three cottages.

It was the fine stone architecture that first attracted Jewson to the Cotswolds and in his reminiscences of that 1907 sketching tour he highlights such features as the richly carved vases and moulded caps of the piers at Cassey Compton and the unconscious beauty of traditional workmanship in the bridges over the River Eye at Lower Slaughter [fig. 45]. And so the principal aim of his own later architectural work, he says, was to produce buildings that had good manners, that did not give offence and that were at home in the landscape.

The arrival of Gimson and the Barnsleys must have had a considerable impact on Sapperton both visually and socially, for not only were their own houses built, but the village hall, a gift of Lady Bathurst, was built by Ernest Barnsley in 1913 and at the west end of the village a pair of cottages was built in 1900 for £400 the pair. Skilled cabinet-makers were brought into the workshop at Daneway and apprenticeships were made available

45. STONE BRIDGES ACROSS THE RIVER EYE AT LOWER SLAUGHTER

for local young men with aptitude. So Edward Gardiner at Daneway sawmill was taught the skills of making ladder-back chairs and the wheelwright's yard below the church was where Alfred Bucknell, son of the Tunley blacksmith Billy Bucknell, had his own smithy making high quality metal goods—firedogs and candleholder sconces from polished steel, as well as hinges and window catches. Richard Harrison, the wheelwright, provided the local wood used in furniture-making. Hill House Farm was leased for accommodating unmarried craftsmen and much employment in the district was created for workers in stone, wood and metal.

The literature suggests that the newcomers integrated well into village life, though their relatively affluent background as the younger sons of prosperous businessmen and their cultured tastes and idealism, stressing the dignity of manual work and the value of community life, would have caused some social distinctiveness.

Jewson generalises on the different outlooks of the residents of Sapperton and those of Oakridge on the other side of the valley, where he had lived for a while before his marriage to Mary Barnsley, daughter of Ernest. Sapperton people shopped in Cirencester. As tenants of the Bathurst estate, usually held on a three life system, they lived under the shadow of Cirencester Park. They had a conservative outlook. Oakridge in contrast originated as a squatter settlement on common land. Here people owned their houses, shopped in Stroud and were independent-minded and radical. They vigorously opposed the enclosure of the commons and were prepared to burn down the pest house which Stroud council wished to use as a smallpox isolation centre. This distinction was seen as far back as the seventeenth century when the royalist family of Pooles entertained Charles I at their manor house in 1644, whereas the Hancox at Daneway were parliamentarians, and it has been suggested that the high tower at Daneway was built to accommodate Cromwell. And employees of the Pooles would have had different loyalties to those in the Oakridge and Stroud area, where the woollen industry was feeling the stress of Dutch competition that was being encouraged by the king.

Today the former squatter settlements have a more disorganised and piecemeal layout with less old property than the compact nucleated villages where church and manor house dominate. In Sapperton's case the manor house has gone and some low mounds of rubble and an unusually flat square of grass indicating the former bowling green are the only visible remains. Jewson informs us that the ornate oak panelling at the ends of the pews and the musicians gallery in the church, and the carved stonework of Alfred's Hall, a folly in Cirencester Park, were taken from the manor house when it was demolished in the mid-eighteenth century. The Kip engraving of 1712 displayed in the church shows its former dominating presence.

At weekends Jewson enjoyed walks in the neighbourhood of Sapperton, mostly with Gimson in the early years and later with family and friends. Typical routes were along the Frome to its source at Brimpsfield; along the Salt Way to Winstone and Elkstone, or deviating to the Duntisbournes; along the canal towpath towards Stroud and over Tarlton Downs to Hasleton. He mentions the churches, the distinguished buildings, the wildlife and the people he met on those walks. Old village characters at Sapperton in the pre-First World War years are fondly remembered, and also the visitors who came to the workshops. One of the pupils Gimson taught was Walter Gissing, whose uncle and guardian Algernon Gissing wrote *A Footpath Way in Gloucestershire*. Work at Iles Farm brought him into contact with Max Beerbohm, Alfred Manning and John Drinkwater, all friends of the Rothensteins for whom he was working. His friendship with Frederick Griggs took him frequently to Chipping Campden and the two worked together on various restorations for the Campden Trust. He mentions other work—on the tower of Magdalen College, Oxford, the church at Salle in Norfolk and the priest's house at Muchelney in Somerset.

But Sapperton was his home. A modest place of leisurely pace which held for him rich memories and for which he had a warm affection. Here, like Gimson before him, he was at peace with himself and with the world, and from which he viewed the surrounding countryside looking at its wildlife and scenery and especially at the seemliness, proportion and quality of workmanship in its buildings. In all of this he was strongly influenced by his early craftsmen friends.

Places to visit: Sapperton for houses, church and graves, site of old manor north of the church. Daneway Bank and Siccaridge Wood for flora and wildlife. Owlpen and Rodmarton Manors. Cheltenham Museum for furniture.

Ivor Gurney

Seeing the Special in the Ordinary

Collected poems and letters, from 1917

Ivor Gurney is now Gloucestershire's most celebrated First World War poet and during his time in the trenches he also became a compulsive letter writer. In addition, he is well known for the music he wrote for songs and he always thought of himself primarily as a musician. He was born in 1890, at 3 Queen's Street, Gloucester, a street that has since disappeared. Soon afterwards the family moved to 19 Barton Street, where his father continued with his work as a tailor. His father was a quiet, gentle man, but his mother was considered harsh and nagging, and from his teens Gurney was not at ease at home. He sensed a degree of hostility and a lack of sympathy for his highfaluting ideas and strongly held opinion of his merit. In 1913 he suffered a nervous breakdown. Following initial rejection on the grounds of eye sight, he joined the Gloucester Reserve Battalion in 1915 and endured many months of trench warfare. Somehow he retained sufficient detachment from all around him to concentrate his mind on songs and poems. In September 1917 he was gassed and this, or shellshock, brought him back to 'Blighty' and he convalesced in Northumberland and Scotland. He was eventually discharged from the army in 1918 and after a number of temporary forms of employment in different places, he was committed to the asylum at Barnwood House in Gloucester and then in 1922 transferred to Dartford Mental Hospital, where he died in 1937, aged 47. He was buried at Twigworth Church, where the Revd Alfred Cheesman, who was his godfather and had befriended him since his boyhood, was the vicar. It is likely that he suffered from paranoid schizophrenia. He described himself as 'being full of unsatisfied longings' and thought he was being tortured by wireless and electricity. During his later asylum years his faculties were dulled but in the period 1913–1926 he wrote nearly nine hundred poems, of which about three hundred are thought to be viable.

At a younger age he was a great walker, covering many miles, often at night, sleeping rough in a barn or under a hedge. He was sharply aware of nature and sensitive to its beauty [fig. 46]. Ordinary things were seen from unusual perspectives. Gloucester and its setting was his first love and whether writing from France, or Northumberland, or Kent, his poems again and again express this. He wrote that the purpose of his poems was to

46. A COTSWOLD
LANE IN MAY

publicise the beauty of Gloucester, to make Gloucester people think about their county, and later that he hoped to make a little money by describing Gloucestershire's beauty.

Throughout he was encouraged in his music and poetry by his friends. These included Alfred Cheesman and the Misses Emily and Margaret Hunt of 54 Wellington Street, Gloucester, Miss Marion Scott, secretary of the Royal College of Music where Gurney studied first under Stanford and then under Vaughan Williams, the family of Arthur Chapman of High Wycombe, several First World War poets, including Edmund Blunden who edited a collection of his poems, and especially by his old boyhood friends, Will Harvey of Minsterworth and Herbert Howells of Lydney. Most of his surviving letters were written to Marion Scott, who not only stored the letters but also oversaw the publication of his two early collections of poems—*Severn and Somme* 1917 and *War's Embers* 1919.

Gurney read extensively, often recommending books to his friends. During and after his war years poetry dominated his reading and his letters reveal his appreciation of Walt Whitman, Rupert Brooke and Laurence Binyon. His own poems have been compared to those of Gerard Manley Hopkins 'of crazy precious diction'. He wrote 'A poem is a collection of words having inexplicable significance giving one vision and vistas'. He often omitted words and, while in the trenches, wrote rapidly in a pocket notebook with no time for correction. However, his later poems were reworked and extensively reshaped. Blunden described his style as gnarled and commented on his merciless intensity of spirit. Robert Bridges wrote that his taste was naturally very severe and artistic. Gurney himself referred to his poems as sincere, true, interesting and original, but on seeing some in print for the first time was struck by their thinness, futility and egoism.

He was described as an awkward, bespectacled and shambling man, intractable and opinionated but with an infectious enthusiasm, guileless charm and good humour.

Many of his poems and letters refer to the First World War, to the mud of the battle field, 'mud sticking closer than a flag seller', 'mud rotting the soul', to the quality of character of his fellow soldiers from the Gloucestershire and Welsh regiments, to the cold, tiredness, boredom, waste and hunger and to his desire to return to England—though he had a fatalistic view of danger. One of the most noteable poems is 'To his love', a response to the news that his old friend Will Harvey was reported missing. Yet again and again his thoughts turn back to Gloucestershire, to the riverside villages of Maisemore, Minsterworth and Framilode, to Crickley and Cranham on the Cotswolds, to the westward views to May Hill and the Malverns and above all to Gloucester.

Gurney was a town boy and until taking up his scholarship at the Royal College of Music in 1911, had lived mainly in Barton Street. As can be appreciated from the few remaining fine bow-fronted houses, Barton Street had been a leading residential street in Gloucester, but by the early twentieth century was busy with small family shops selling essential goods, 'small shops of multimiscellany'. The Cross, where the four main streets meet, was the hub of city life, with people coming in from the country to shop, to market, or to do business, while the port received ships from near and far. Gurney comments from France of his memory of the character shown on the peoples' faces, on his sense of Gloucester's history, and on the dominance of the cathedral.

> Who says 'Gloucester' sees a tall
> Fairfashioned shape of stone arise,
> That changes with the changing skies
> From joy to gloom funereal,
> Then quick again to joy; and sees
> Those four most ancient ways come in
> To mix their folk and dust and din
> With the keen scent of the sea breeze

47. GLOUCESTER DOCKS AND THE MARINERS' CHURCH, WHERE GURNEY WAS ORGANIST
FOR A WHILE

Today, there have been valiant attempts to attract attention to the city's history with wall plaques and murals, and the base of the Roman wall which ran under Gurney's birthplace has been exposed to view in Eastgate Street. The former Barton Street has changed character to provide leisure facilities, fast food and ethnic goods, the port area caters mainly for leisure and tourists [fig. 47] and the Cross is no longer the busiest part of the city. Yet the Cathedral still dominates the skyline. Although a chorister and articled to Dr Brewer, the cathedral organist, and familiar with the massive pillars and delicate stonework of the cathedral, it was the square-shaped, dominating presence of the cathedral that so impressed Gurney.

He often viewed it from Maisemore to which he walked every Sunday evening with his father to visit his grandmother. From a closer viewpoint its great tower appeared as 'masses of stone gone slender as a silver birch, upwards in dazzle to an arching azure' [fig. 48]. The changing light upon the cathedral, sometimes joyful, some-times gloomy, with the white clouds hanging above the tower, de-lighted him.

After the war, as his mental problems in-creased, Gurney worked for a while in a tax office in College Court and wrote about the house 'Georgian with a stairway up to the roof and banisters of carved and curving grace'. But like all his employment it was short lived—a mere twelve weeks.

48. GLOUCESTER CATHEDRAL 'MASSES OF STONE GONE SLENDER AS A SILVER BIRCH'

After his discharge from the army and a

49. VIEW WEST FROM CRICKLEY HILL, ABOVE DRYHILL FARM WHERE GURNEY
WORKED FOR A TIME

brief return to the Royal College of Music, he took a labourer's job at Dry Hill Farm, above Shurdington, and so renewed his acquaintance with Crickley Hill. 'Work was dreer, five shillings a week, but O the beauty of the place'. Many poems refer to Crickley [fig. 49]. Sometimes the flora of the escarpment, scabious, harebells and bee orchids attract his notice, at other times it is the wind causing the flowers to nod all day and at gale force bending the beech trees, or the tracks of rabbits, or the call of the curlew and the swift flight of the kite. The view westward over buttercup meadows, 'uncounted gold strewn in green meadows', with their white hedges when hawthorn is in flower, 'foam on green waves', and the passage of clouds like fleets of ships sailing up the Severn valley, backed by May Hill and the Malverns, especially in the setting sun, inspired his poetry. He wrote of his thoughts while working here, felling a hundred year old ash tree for firewood, hoeing turnips, or helping with the plough. From time to time a Roman coin or a piece of pottery was unearthed and he reflected on life and thought in Roman times. He felt some affinity to Roman soldiers with his own experience of war in a foreign land. He enjoyed the loneliness of the hill where few people came, where the steep gradient kept the traffic away and where the bare rock exposures from earlier quarrying seemed to invite classical inscriptions.

Kites (possibly he meant kestrels) and curlew have gone; the status of the hill as a country park, lungs for the people of Gloucester and Cheltenham, has shattered the quietness; excavations and information boards of the important Iron Age hillfort have displaced the archaeological significance of the Dry Hill Roman villa; the modern A419 carries an endless stream of heavy lorries up Crickley Hill and the view in the middle

50. THE URBAN SPRAWL OF GLOUCESTER, VIEWED FROM CHURCHDOWN HILL.

distance is dominated by the urban sprawl of Gloucester [fig. 50]. But there are still the flowers on the grassy slopes and the wind and the skyscape and the magnificent sunsets, 'huge bonfires of glory'.

> The orchis, trefoil, harebells nod all day,
> High above Gloucester and the Severn Plain.
> Few come here where the curlew ever and again
> Cries faintly, and no traveller makes stay

Another well-loved place in his early poems and wartime letters was Framilode. Framilode, 'part of the stuff of me, ineradicable, not to be removed', was a magical place with its tides and elvers, a place where Gurney and Harvey sailed together. Here the Stroudwater Canal joined the Severn and the old lock-keeper is portrayed in a poem which praises his depth of knowledge of river-birds and fish, of wind and tides.

Minsterworth, with its smell of apple orchards and its elm trees, the home of Will Harvey's family, was another favourite, and so was Cranham, 'autumn Cranham with its boom of colour'.

Gurney's thought has been described as stuttering but he had a clear-sighted awareness of nature and noticed the ordinary things that others missed. 'One comes across the strangest things on walks', such as monastic stones re-used in modern buildings, overgrown brick kilns, old mounting stones, the contrasting skyline of the different roads climbing up the Cotswold escarpment, and the way skylarks 'hang shaking' as they sing.

51. DEERHURST NEAR THE SEVERN 'A TALL THING CLEAN AND POISED'

He noticed the changing colour of road surfaces through the seasons—the azure April sky (azure again) reflected in puddles, the bleached dust in summer and the varied browns of autumn leaves.

He was fascinated by the shapes of buildings such as the Saxon church at Deerhurst 'a tall thing clean and poised like any boy walker' [fig. 51], or Tewkesbury Abbey 'that square thing, name of stone and battle', near to where the green Avon joins the brown Severn, and also by the shapes of landforms such as Leckhampton 'elbow' and 'jagged Malvern'.

His perception of the Cotswold towns contrasts with that of other writers of the time. Gurney was never sentimental or romantic with regard to these. So the poem on Northleach 'that jewel, white stone and green foliage, breadth in the street, dignity in dwelling, on the Roman way standing' ends with the realism 'the body, as the spirit, demands natural poetry, tea on the high Cotswolds—at an inn, noble from the wealth of corn'. This is a reference to the Wheatsheaf Inn. And he is not unaware of the fragile economy of Chipping Camden 'only at certain times the tourists go there, and the town lives feebly on unemployment pay, housed in the old gettings of wool ware'. But of other towns across the country he wrote 'England is cancered and defiled by ugly towns and commodious villas, born of vulgarity, sluggish liver, greed, and all uncharitableness'.

Since he often walked at night, the sounds of the night, the silhouettes of trees and buildings, the moon and the stars are often referred to both in poems and in letters. Many stars are mentioned and he drew comfort from the fact that the stars seen above the battle fields of northern France were the same as he had seen in Gloucestershire. Then night gave way to dawn, 'smudgy dawn scarfed with military colours'.

Gurney has been described as a sky poet as a result of his interest in sunset, dawn, stars and clouds, but even in this his skies are often 'earthed'. So the 'clouds on patrol' patrol the Severn valley and those caused by rising currents of air are formed along the Cotswold edge and mists form over the water meadows by the river. Arcturus, one of the many stars he names, is over May Hill.

Gurney's religious faith was shaken in the First World War, but he had a profound theology. He concludes his poem on Gloucester, 'The Old City', with these lines:—

> If one must die for England, Fate has given
> Generously indeed, for we have known
> Before our time, the air and skies of Heaven
> And Beauty more than common have been shown,
> And with our last fight fought, our last strife striven
> We shall enter unsurprised into our own.

Few could express their love of Gloucestershire more eloquently.

Places to visit: There is a plaque marking his birthplace in Queen's Walk, Gloucester, a memorial in Gloucester Cathedral on a pillar by the north aisle and a recent stained glass window commemorating his life and work in St Mary de Lode Church. He was for a time organist at the Mariners' Church at the docks. Fine views, well loved by Gurney, are from Sandhurst Hill looking down on Ashleworth, from Barrow Hill towards Framilode and all around, from Robinswood and Cooper's Hill and especially from the country park on Crickley Hill looking over Dry Hill Farm to the Severn valley and the Malverns beyond. One almost expects to meet Harvey and Gurney when walking down one of the lanes or footpaths from Minsterworth to the Severn and then along to the church, particularly in Maytime.

F.W. HARVEY

SEEING WITH THE SOUL
AS WELL AS THE EYE

Collected poems, from 1916

In the south transept of Gloucester Cathedral is a memorial plaque to Will Harvey. It states simply 'Frederick William Harvey D.C.M. Soldier and Poet of Gloucestershire 1888–1957' and then a quotation from his writings 'He loved the vision of this world and found it good'.

Harvey was born at Murrell's End, Hartpury, but the family soon moved to a farm at Minsterworth, The Redlands. Here, on a traditional mixed farm. his father specialised in rearing Shire horses to sell to local farmers and for brewers' drays, and here Harvey spent his childhood and youth. It was a place to which he returned whenever possible in later life. Minsterworth with its red earth, its water meadows, its orchards and the Severn was home to him. After schooling at the King's School, Gloucester and Rossall School in Lancashire, he was articled to a Gloucester solicitor in St John's Lane. He found the work tedious and in later life was only really interested in unusual cases, particularly if they involved clients who, he felt, had been shabbily treated. He never prospered as a solicitor. At the outbreak of the First World War he joined the Gloucestershire Regiment, was awarded the D.C.M. and taken as a prisoner of war. He wrote his best poetry in custody and, like those of his friend Ivor Gurney, his poems were often nostalgic reflections on Gloucestershire. After the war, on resuming his work, he took some time to settle. He married Anne, an Irish nurse, and following moves to Cranham and Broadoak, they eventually made their home at the old School House, Yorkley, where they lived in poverty and some squalor. Harvey was buried at Minsterworth parish church [fig. 52] under a yew tree by the Severn. It has been fittingly observed that he did for Gloucestershire what Kipling and Belloc did for Sussex and Housman for Shropshire.

Many of his nature poems are simple, often humorous and lyrical. They can be read with a chuckle and a twinkle in the eye. He said he had been taught to look at nature by Richard Jefferies, to 'observe as a poet rather than as a naturalist, to see with the soul as well as with the eye'. Some poems refer with respect and gratitude to his mother, a major influence on his life, and others to easily overlooked local characters like Charlie

52. ST PETER'S
CHURCH,
MINSTERWORTH
BY THE SEVERN.
HARVEY'S GRAVE
IS HERE

the Black. Some are written in Gloucestershire dialect. Other poems, particularly those reflecting on his war and captivity experiences, touch on the deeper issues of life and on a faith that can sustain even in those terrible conditions.

One of the key elements in the landscape of Minsterworth, 'queen of riverside places', is the Severn [fig. 53]. The incoming tide is fronted by the famous bore, which is most impressive with the spring tides and a north-east wind. Harvey describes 'the sleek brown skin, the mighty rush, the angry head upreared'. It arrives at Minsterworth with a white foaming front followed by a series of waves, like a lumpy ribbon of water, and with a rumbling noise, which becomes a roar as the bore passes and travels upstream at about twelve miles an hour. The muddy turbulent water continues to rise for about another hour and then at the turn of the tide there is silence in the full river. 'You can hear your watch's tick'.

In the season of Lent the tide brings in the elvers, not so many today but then millions. The young eels move up river after their three year journey from the Sargasso Sea. They

53. THE
SEVERN AT
MINSTERWORTH
IN THE EARLY
MORNING

swim against the tide and keep to the water's edge where they have been caught at night for centuries. Hundreds of fishermen waded into the shallow water with their lanterns and nets to catch this local delicacy.

> 'Millions, billions of glassy bright
>   Little wormy fish
>   Chewed-string fish,
>   Slithery dithery fish
> In the dead of the night.'

Salmon were also caught, often in putcheons—wicker basket traps—set in the water at night. Few are caught today but several old brick fishermens' huts are still standing along this stretch of the Severn [fig. 54]. Harvey and Gurney jointly owned a small boat, the 'Dorothy', and enjoyed sailing down to Bollow Pool and Framilode [fig. 55]. Even from distant viewpoints such as Painswick Beacon, it is the Severn like a 'silver eel' that attracts Harvey's attention.

The agricultural land use at Minsterworth was determined by soil conditions. So the low-lying meadows by the Severn and along the small streams, where flooding occurs in the winter and the water table is always close to the surface, were for cattle grazing. Shorthorns and Gloucesters were the most popular breeds of dairy cattle then and he writes 'Gloucestershire meadows lie speckled red with herds'. Today the colouring is more likely to be the black and white of Friesians or Friesian cross-bred cattle. Better drained land has wider potential and here wheat, barley and beans were grown. Of the fertile soils on the Keuper Marl north of the village he writes 'the springing wheat which like green water washes the red old earth of Minsterworth'. Most farms were mixed and their

54. AN OLD SALMON FISHERMEN'S HUT AT MINSTERWORTH

55. FRAMILODE, A FAVOURITE SAILING DESTINATION OF HARVEY AND GURNEY

layout across the varied types of soil encouraged this variety of interest. Gloucester was the market for their produce.

More significant for him than the field crops and livestock were the orchards. Several poems recall blossom time and its bees, perry and cider orchards, fruit picking and the silhouette of winter fruit trees at sunset. Frost is one of the main problems for fruit growers, particularly frosts occurring between blossom time and the setting of the fruit. In the spring there is colder air over the Severn so blossom time is delayed, and the river encourages the free drainage of cold air from the slopes of the low hills rather than allowing it to stagnate. Both reduce frost damage. So Minsterworth has long been an orchard area. Cats Heads, producing very large cookers, Ribston Pippin and Skyrmes Kernel were common apple trees. Most orchards were for cider apples and each variety gave its own distinctive flavour to the cider. Thomas Rudge writing in 1805 said that the strength of the liquor depended on the strength of the soil, clay gave the richest and most powerful cider, sandy soils gave thinner cider. The soils around Minsterworth were ideal—and not only for apples. Pears too were grown and pear trees produced fruit for longer periods. At fifty years apple trees were producing 10–15 bushels and continued to do so till the century was reached, but pears continued far longer and Rudge mentions a three hundred year old pear tree at Minsterworth producing 340 gallons of perry.

Farms with larger orchards had horse cider mills, where the apples were pulped by a four foot diameter stone runner that was pulled by the horse round a circular stone trough. Smaller orchards were served by hand mills. Pulp was then transferred to the cider press, where, wrapped in hair cloth, the 'cheeses' were pressed and the juice extracted. This was then stored in casks. Some cider or perry was sold and sent up and down the Severn, but much was consumed on the farm. Turner, writing as far back as 1794, says the farm labourer's allowance was not less than a gallon a day all year round and two gallons at harvest.

The acreage under apples and pears has greatly diminished with changes in marketing policy and legislation standards and with rising labour costs, but blossom time is still noticeable. Old cider presses are often seen in farmyards. At the National Trust garden at Westbury Court a number of the old fruit varieties are grown.

> 'I love the tangled orchards blowing bright
> With clouds of apple blossom, and the red
> Ripe fruit that hangs a-shining in blue air
> Like rubies hanging in the orchard's hair'.

Around the farm at Redlands were elm trees. 'Heavy elms which held his memories', he wrote in a poem in 1919. And 'Winter trees etched ebony on sunset'. Their winter tracery and unrest in the wind often caught his attention. And so did the flowers of the lanes he frequently walked with Ivor Gurney. 'Pale primrose fires lighting the lane' and the snowy may blossom on the hedgerows.

The horizons from Minsterworth were distinct. To the east the Cotswolds—curving, high and cool, like a blade drawn from its scabbard, and with its white quarry scars. To the north-west May Hill, 'a quiet coloured bubble', and beyond the 'jagged Malverns'.

For a brief time soon after their marriage the Harveys lived in a cottage in Cranham woods, in part of what is today Walnut Tree Cottage. Will cycled each day to work in Gloucester and enjoyed the cottage setting in the autumn beech woods. 'Smouldering beech' he called it, appreciating the blood stains on the woodland floor when his back was to the sun and the forms of the trees as he faced it in the evening light.

When his work moved to Newnham, the Harveys rented a pair of converted railway carriages on the banks of the Severn at Broadoak as their home [fig. 56]. While here he wrote a poem on the first signs of spring—a wisp of hay in the river indicating the last of the winter feed for cattle on the meadows, a fresh green hawthorn leaf floating on the water and a skiff with salmon nets. Part of the old carriage house is now preserved in the railway museum at Winchcombe.

56. THE OLD RAILWAY CARRIAGES THE HARVEYS LIVED IN AT BROADOAK, NOW IN THE RAILWAY MUSEUM, WINCHCOMBE

57. 'FROM TROUBLES OF
THE WORLD
I TURN TO DUCKS'.

The Harvey's finally bought the old school house at Yorkley from which Will initially travelled to work in Lydney but later, as income declined, he worked from home. Sometimes he travelled by train between Lydney and Coleford, a slow loitering journey. A rail journey that kept pace with a butterfly and which ensured an escape from the bustle of life to …

'Fade into glint of fern and flower,
Where quarries gleam and foxgloves tower,
And for one lovely lazy hour
Forget …'

Several collections of Harvey's poems were published in his lifetime. The earlier collections with their promise of more to come were successful commercially. Some poems such as 'Ducks' [fig. 57], 'Ghosts' and 'The Bugler' became widely known. Others expressed a mystic strain as, like Gurney, he thought of his Gloucestershire roots.

'O Lord, within my heart for ever
Set this sweet shape of land and winding river,
That I may taste their comfort till I die
And feed upon them in Eternity'.

Harvey probably never fulfilled his potential as a poet but he remains the most important for Gloucestershire, its poet laureate.

Places to visit: Minsterworth Church for the lectern—the great yellow bird as perceived by a child. Harvey's grave near the east end of the church.

Walks beside the Severn both at Minsterworth and on the opposite bank at Elmore for the river, the bore and the orchards.

His favourite view points were Churchdown Hill, May Hill and Painswick Beacon.

ALGERNON GISSING

WALKING IN THE NORTH COTSWOLDS
A HUNDRED YEARS AGO

The Footpath Way in Gloucestershire, 1924

In 1924 Dent published this small book. It is a collection of savoured memories and reflections on walks and conversations in the North Cotswolds in the last decade or so of the nineteenth century, when Gissing lived in a cottage on the green at Willersey. It begins with a climb up through the October mist to the clear sunshine above Saintbury church and the memories of his first meeting with William Smith.

William Smith, whose photograph taken by Henry Taunt is now reproduced in the Saintbury parish notes [fig. 58], was parish clerk from 1834 to 1901, sexton, violinist, bell-ringer and road-mender, and was Gissing's chief informant from the time of their first meeting in 1887 to Smith's death in 1910. He is buried in the churchyard. Although an intelligent man, educated with the family of the kindly vicar, and interested in the past events of the locality, he had little appreciation of the natural beauty of the area. Its scenery and wildlife were taken for granted and he had no concern for their protection from what Gissing calls the inroads of mechanical efficiency. The fact that this attitude was typical of the villagers bothered Gissing, as it seemed to reflect a deficiency in the schooling they had received. Clearly a sense of beauty was felt by the builders of the churches and manor houses, but somehow this

58. WILLIAM SMITH, GISSING'S INFORMANT,
PHOTOGRAPHED BY HENRY TAUNT

59. BUCKLE STREET FOR 'PEEPS INTO THE COTSWOLDS'

had been lost. Like Henry Warren, he thought that local history should be in the school curriculum and he suggested that every parish should have a large-scale map displayed in the village school, or in a conspicuous public place, to show footpaths, field names and features of interest. There would then be, he thought, more resistence to the dumping of old pots and pans, bottles and other waste in the hedgerows and on the trackways, to the blocking of footpaths by barbed wire, and to the wanton destruction of all obstacles to the latest utilitarian development.

He followed the many footpaths around Saintbury and Willersey, over the hills to Chipping Campden, and south-west to Winchcombe and beyond. One can easily trace his movements with the aid of a 1:25,000 Ordnance Survey map. In the 1890s most lanes off the low road (now the B4632) were still repaired with stones from local quarries. In dry summers they were white and dusty, but in wet periods were orange coloured (both Gibbs and Evans make similar observations). Buckle Street [fig. 59], the early through route from Alcester via Bidford-on-Avon to the Fosse Way at Bourton-on-the-Water, was followed for 'peeps into the real spirit of these hills'. It was overgrown in the Vale at the foot of the escarpment, but wide and open on the wolds and rich in flowers. Another old routeway that mounted the escarpment above Hailes was the Saltway, along which, in medieval times, pack horses carried salt from Droitwich to Lechlade. Boats then transported the salt to London for preserving meat and fish. Gissing mentions the place names incorporating 'salt' and the manorial records that confirm this old route. All the spring-line villages have old tracks that link the wold and vale portions of their parishes and along these sheep were moved between summer and winter pasture. Those tracks with gentler gradients, or of more than parochial significance, have become modern roads, but many have remained as greenways. Gissing thought that all these villages were best approached and viewed from the roads above them. In the late nineteenth century landowners did not object to considerate walkers crossing their fields but by the 1920s access was much more restricted and churches were normally locked.

Every parish had its quarry from which stone was extracted for the village buildings, for some of the field boundary walls, and for the roads. Quarries varied in size and in the quality of the building stone. As the Inferior Oolite outcrops at the top of the escarpment, the spring-line villages had their quarries here. In the cases of Weston, Saintbury and Willersey, where the parishes taper to the south, the quarries were almost adjacent to one another. None of these quarries is worked today, but the Broadway Hill Quarry above Fish Hill, is still productive. William Smith frequently worked at the Saintbury quarry where he was paid 10d per cubic yard for stone breaking. For roof slates a different type of sandy limestone was required, and this was obtained from Guiting or Eyford. Gissing quotes Dawber on the way the slates were prepared. Pendle (the mined Stonesfield Slate) was dug out and spread on the ground in October, so that the moisture in the rock could freeze during frosty nights and thus loosen the layers of the rock. Then with the use of a slate cutter, the tiles were cut to the various shapes and sizes required for the traditional vernacular slate roofs. Old quarries were havens for wildlife and, as the quarry faces and floors weather, plants colonise the rock waste.

Over fifty species of wild flowers are mentioned in the book, some of meadow and woodland, some of hedgerow and wayside, and many of the old quarries. Several flowers are given more extended comment. The pasque flower was rare even then and Gissing thought it worth preserving. It was found on the open pasture between the thorn bushes in Barnsley Warren. He mentions it flowering in May, after the April snow melt. The spectacular combination of cowslips and early purple orchis in the field below Gunn's Cottages [fig. 60], William Smith's childhood home, only occurred on one occasion in the years he visited the area. The heather and gorse, growing on a residual acidic soil

60. GUNN'S COTTAGES, THE CHILDHOOD HOME
OF WILLIAM SMITH

on Cleeve Hill, surrounded by calcareous plants such as thyme, rockrose, tormentil and scabious, interested him, as did the woolly thistles in the quarry, whose seed heads were so attractive to goldfinches. Of trees, the elm was widespread on the clay lowland and along the village streets, beech marked the parish boundary on the hill and at Spring Hill beech was planted in clumps to represent battalions of soldiers in the Battle of Waterloo. It was quite common for the sons of landed gentry returning from the Napoleonic wars to plant trees in this way. Larch plantations were less welcomed replacements for beech on the wolds, but there were still acres of old thorn trees with their grotesque and weird outlines on the hillsides at Kineton and Eyford.

Gissing compares the escarpment parishes to an opened scroll. On the hill the land was cultivated with barley and oats, and with root crops such as mangels, turnips and swedes for sheep fodder. There were also fields of clover and Gissing said fifteen percent of the Cotswolds was growing sainfoin, giving a warm, cheerful, pink colour to the landscape. He quotes Cobbett's reference to ugly, stone walled, square fields, 'cheerless, miserable and abominable', but does not concur. The slopes were of pasture or woodland and contained the quarries. Then around the grey nucleated villages at the foot of the escarpment were the orchards, and beyond them were the cattle pastures and wheat fields. With these different components each parish had variety and colour and could be largely self-sufficient.

The dates of the Parliamentary Enclosure Acts for some of the parishes are given— Snowshill 1760, Willersey 1767, Condicote 1777, and Weston 1850. Land close to the villages had been enclosed at much earlier dates, and some twenty of the old field names are given. The later parliamentary enclosures related to the more distant parts of the parishes. These enclosures shattered village life. Cottagers who had been able to graze a few animals on the common land could no longer do so. Some farmers moved out of the villages to their newly allocated blocks of land. The old wild charm of the hills was lost, rural sports like coursing were stopped, and Gissing suggests that enclosure, more than anything else, broke communities. It is not clear if he was merely expressing the opinion of the day, or reporting local evidence. Further loss of old grassland came with the First World War policy of ploughing up pasture and then the conversion of Willersey Hill into a golf course.

Traditionally, orchards had formed part of the landscape but the old moss and lichen covered trees were giving way to the more carefully tended commercial orchards. It was a cider and perry drinking area and so each October the fruit trees were vigorously shaken and the fallen fruit piled into heaps on the ground, or loaded on to the yellow farm wagons. Like Warren, Gissing mentions the scent of rotting apples wafting on the south-west wind. The cider mill was at the Manor Farm and here the apples were pulped and the pips crushed by the stone wheel turned by a pony. As in other parts of the county, the cider allowance was normally eight quarts a day at harvest and haymaking (notice the allowance was double at this time!). The casks for storing these vast quantities of cider usually held 110 gallons, but some held 400 or 500 gallons. The strength of the cider was best conserved in the larger barrels. The drink was said to be anti-arthritic and an old writer is quoted saying that cider 'procures a good appetite, helps the digestion, cheers the heart and revives the spirit, and is less hurtful than beer in its operation on the brain'! Cider was not the only drink. There was also cowslip wine, grape wine and mead made from the washings of honeycomb.

The diverse habitats, ranging from breezy wold to sheltered hollow and including the different types of farmland, encouraged bird life. There were no gamekeepers in these parishes so kestrels, sparrow hawks and owls were unmolested. The little owl had recently arrived in the area and the redstart was disappearing. Thirty species of bird are mentioned.

Very perceptive comments are made about the different types of village. The northern wold villages, such as Snowshill, Cutsdean and Condicote, high and exposed, are contrasted with those further south in the valleys, such as the Guitings, which were more wooded and sheltered. Green villages, such as Willersey and Condicote, are noted. Green villages are often found in border areas where pastoral farming was important. Here livestock could be brought on to the green for defence against cattle rustling. Greens are also characteristic of villages which had a strong sense of community, so that no private dwellings were allowed on the green, maybe an inn, or blacksmith's forge, a village pump house and in latter years a school, but no houses. The green at Condicote was divided into allotments in the late nineteenth century. At Willersey, the Blue Bell Inn, the smithy, the pond and the saw pit were on the green, and on the 24th June, at the end of haymaking, the fair arrived for the annual village wake. The village green was also the place for games.

Another distinction Gissing notes is between the squire and squireless villages. Villages with a squire were estate villages. Housing was of good quality since there was capital available for repairs, work was on the estate so there was less scope for private enterprise, and the population was selected for its suitability for employment on the estate. Social facilities depended largely on the benevolence of the squire and there was a strong influence on voting behaviour and on church attendance. The squireless villages were open, more populated and independent. Housing was often poorer and non-conformist chapels were common. Income from a smallholding was supplemented by other work, and craftsmen and tradesmen were more likely to be found in these villages. There was scope for initiative and self interest. This nineteenth century contrast is still seen in the fabric of today's villages. Willersey was a squireless village, while Aston-sub-Edge had a squire. Gissing regretted the passing of the old landed gentry who cared for their estates and had the capital to maintain them.

Because the villages were close to each other, about one mile apart at the scarp foot, there was easy contact between them. Festivals brought them together, craftsmen such as wheelwrights and shoemakers linked them, and friendly rivalry sustained their interest in one another. Animosity was more likely between vale and wold villages. Something not quite in keeping was 'of the hill', or 'from Stow way', and no doubt this was reciprocated.

61. DOVER'S HILL, THE SITE OF THE COTSWOLD OLYMPICS

One of William Smith's treasured possessions was a piccolo which had belonged to the last hayward of a neighbouring village. Smith's interest in music-making and bell-ringing provided information on the time before the harmonium and hymn singing became popular in churches. Then the anthem was played by the quartet of village musicians with violin, cello, flute and clarinet. However, when music was required for social events, a fifth person was added to the quartet to help consume the excess liquor provided for the music makers! Most of the churches had a peel of five or six bells, and these were rung not only for the Sunday services but on many other occasions. For example at 5 a.m. on St Thomas' Day, 21st December, to mark the beginning of the Christmas season, or at 6 a.m. on 29th May for Restoration Day, or joyfully to welcome in the New Year. Bells are the 'natural voice of the countryside'.

At the top of the escarpment above Aston-sub-Edge is Dover's Hill [fig. 61]. Here from 1604 was the location of the Cotswold Olympic Games. These were founded by Robert Dover in association with Endymion Porter, who was born in the manor house at Aston-sub-Edge. The Games were held on the Thursday and Friday of Whit Week and included events catering for a wide range of skills. Horse racing over the downs, wrestling, pitching the hammer and bar, handling the pike, walking on hands, country dancing, cudgel playing and shin kicking were examples. Vast crowds, sometimes more than thirty thousand people, gathered on the hill to spectate. By the middle of the nineteenth century, the Games had degenerated and became associated with fighting and the occasion for settling old scores. So the rector closed them in 1851, with a fair measure of local support, and parts of the hill were then enclosed. The Games were recommenced on a smaller scale for the Festival of Britain in 1951 and continue to the present day.

Close to Dover's Hill, by the lane from Broadway, is the Kiftsgate Stone [fig. 62], which marks the site of meetings of the Kiftsgate Hundred. Near this spot is a fine view to the east over Chipping Campden. In the evening light the town is a golden grey. Gissing refers to the sheep grey of Cumbria and the sombre grey and silver grey of Yorkshire, but here the iron content of the stone gives the golden colour. He mentions the market charter and the fairs of the town and the contribution to its prosperity of such men as William Grevel, wool merchant, John Fereby, founder of the Grammar School, and Sir Baptist Hicks, whose almshouses

62. THE KIFTSGATE STONE

and market hall still stand as important buildings. At one time the wool towns like Chipping Campden were the wealthiest places in England.

Winchcombe is the other historic town he briefly discusses and he describes the way in which the demolition of the great abbey provided stone for the later dwellings. The Corner Cupboard Inn and Rabbit Box Cottage opposite are examples.

From the skilful drystone walling around the original false entrance to the long barrow of Belas Knap—and Gissing deplores the untidy, uncaring waste left by the archaeological excavators—through the fourteenth- and fifteenth-century preaching crosses at Condicote and Saintbury, to the churches, manor houses, farms and cottages, there is

63. VIEW OF
SAINTBURY FROM
WILLERSEY CHURCH.

64. SAINTBURY FROM CASTLE BANK.

much craftsmanship to celebrate. There were still very capable craftsmen in the villages, and he notes how Ernest Gimson tapped the native genius. In fact Gimson himself made the side screen in Saintbury church and there are other features of the Arts and Crafts movement here in the chancel chandelier by C.R. Ashbee and the delicately carved figure of St Nicholas by Alec Miller on the north door.

The whole landscape is celebrated with its mysteriously velvety texture. The view from Willersey church towards Saintbury [fig. 63], or from Castle Bank above Saintbury church [fig. 64], or from Dover's Hill looking over the Vale of Evesham, especially in the clear conditions provided by the unstable air of a north-west wind, are recommended. They are appreciated for their own sake but also for the insight they give into English literature. Gissing says the landscape gives one of the best commentaries on Shakespeare and 'if only as a key to the treasures of our most characteristic literature, the imaginative outlook on our rural life and landscape is indispensable'.

The book is not only homely and sensitive—whether to the scent of hay, the sound of the hurdy-gurdy announcing Willersey wake, the profound damson blue of the Malverns at dusk, or the touch of the stone stile, but it also gives glimpses into a lost past through the memories of the old village clerk and beyond him to those of earlier residents.

Places to visit: Saintbury, especially the church. Willersey. Chipping Campden.

Leonard Clark

The Forest Edge through Childhood Memories

Greenwood, 1962 and *A Fool in the Forest*, 1965

In the 1960s three small collections of autobiographical essays by Leonard Clark were published. The essays contain brief, affectionate descriptions of life on the edge of the Forest of Dean in the first two decades of the twentieth century. He tells us that he was born on Guernsey but from the age of one was fostered by Sarah George at Cinderford. One day in 1906 he was collected at Newnham station from the Paddington–South Wales train and for the next twenty years, or so, lived with Sarah and her three sons in their 1890s stone house off Belle View Road, Cinderford. Sarah's husband, James, had been a forestry worker, but had died young.

Leonard Clark was a pupil at Double View School. This had opened in 1895 for six hundred children under its first headmaster, John Emery. Clark then won a scholarship to Monmouth School and later returned to Double View as a pupil teacher. A university education was too costly for the family but money was provided for him to train at Bangor Normal College. He began teaching in Camberwell and then in 1936 became a school inspector specialising in primary education, English and music. He retired in 1971 and died ten years later at the age of 76.

From his teens he had written poetry and some early examples were printed in the *Forest of Dean Mercury*, the local newspaper. He was given encouragement in this by Will Harvey and had several collections of poems published. He also edited anthologies of poems including, in 1973, a collection of Ivor Gurney's. This chapter is based primarily on *Greenwood* published in 1962 and *A Fool in the Forest* published in 1965.

Cinderford, he wrote, 'had never been a beautiful place and had all the grimness of a Victorian creation. It was a little, grey, drab mining town of unambitious circumstances'. But originally it had been more than a coal mining town [fig. 65].

Although there had been early attempts at using coal in iron-making in the Forest of Dean, these had been unsuccessful until in 1795 the first coke blast furnace was built in Cinderford at the Cinderford Iron Works. This furnace used iron ore, brought down on mule back from the Edge Hill mines to the east, and coke, which had been

65. THE MINER'S STATUE, CINDERFORD

made by charking coal near Broadmoor, a mile north, and brought by canal. In 1835 the Welsh industrialist William Crawshay became involved with the industry and so began his wide-ranging interest in the area, an interest which was carried on by his son Henry. The Crawshays eventually owned the Cinderford Iron Works, the iron mines supplying them at Shakemantle, Buckshaft, St Annal's and Westbury Brook, the coal mines at Lightmoor and Foxes Bridge, and much of the extensive tramway network around Cinderford.

Iron production led to the establishment of local foundries to produce cast iron products from the remelted pig iron. So Upper Bilson, Bilson, Tingle's, Steam Mills, Forest Vale and Heywood Foundries were formed. The Forest Vale Iron Works later produced wire and in 1880 employed 100 men. Several thousand men were also employed in the mines.

The Cinderford Iron Works closed in 1894, being unable to compete in difficult times with production elsewhere, and particularly with the South Wales industry. So iron mining also ceased—at Edge Hill in 1893 and at Shakemantle, Buckshaft and St Annal's in 1899. The Forest Vale Iron Works closed in 1895. Some engineering continued, as with Teague and Chew at Steam Mills, but by the early twentieth century Clark is right to describe Cinderford as a mining town—coal mining that is. There was however a large ironworking legacy still clearly visible.

Cinderford had 'a population of three thousand people, mostly living on the edge of poverty', but was marvellously surrounded by woods and hills. The main street and four side roads had many small shops, and for a few of the shopkeepers descriptions are given of the impression they made on their youthful customer. So for example, reference is made to the two Boud sisters, who kept a high-class confectionary shop, and to the relatively prosperous grocer, Richard Westaway, and to the family butcher, Sam Featherstone. When he made a return visit to Cinderford some forty years later, Clark found many of these shop names unchanged.

Several public houses are mentioned, such as the Globe, where the silver band practised, the Mount Pleasant, Clark's local and the White Hart, near which in the 1890s a client met an escaped circus lion! In fact, of the 115 retail premises in Cinderford listed in the 1919 Kelly's Directory, no less than 35 sold beer, so providing miners with welcome refreshment at the end of their long hours underground.

66. ON THE PATH
TO LONGHOPE

Community life is fondly described from the point of view of an interested onlooker. The atmosphere of intense and longstanding rivalry between exhibitors and the controversial decision-making of the judges at the annual flower show on the Recreation Ground, the splendid band contests in Lydney Park, to which came brass and silver bands from all over the Forest, the church and chapel treats with their teas and games on fixed days in the summer calendar, the boxing match when fighting spread from the ring into the seating area as village loyalty overcame mere spectator interest and the harvest festival displays with the bishop preaching at St Stephen's Church, are vividly recalled. These events together with the wild beast show on the Railway Meadow and the travelling theatre in the Market Yard provided variety and colour to life in Cinderford in the days before mass media entertainment. Some of these observations could have been made of small town community life anywhere in the country at the time but some are specific to the Forest!

Travel opportunities were restricted. Newnham had the nearest main line railway station, but express trains did not stop there. Cinderford station was on a branch line and had limited use for some local journeys. For the journey to Gloucester Walkley's horse brake was used. This service was on Mondays, Wednesdays and Saturdays and took three hours for the downhill journey there and four hours for the slow climb back. It went from Cinderford Bridge to the Spread Eagle Hotel by the old cattle market in Gloucester, with a stop for refreshments at the Bird-in-Hand (now the Severn Bore) below Chaxhill. On other days, as for example for Clark's first visit to the Three Choirs Festival in Gloucester Cathedral for Handel's *Messiah*, which was on a Friday, the fourteen miles had to be walked. The Littledean cricket team also used a horse brake and Clark tells us the journey time from Cinderford to Longhope by this means was two hours each way. Walking was the normal mode of transport and often as quick. Visits were made to friends and family at Pope's Hill, Drybrook, Ruardean and Longhope [fig. 66] and to Newnham for

67. BLOSSOM TIME AT POPE'S HILL

68. LOOKING NORTH EAST FROM DOUBLE VIEW ON TO THE MIST-SHROUDED UMBRELLA SHAPE
OF CHESTNUTS WOOD

picnics by the river. For very special occasions the train was taken over the Severn Bridge to Sharpness and the journey continued by paddle steamer to Weston for a day on the sand.

From the top of Littledean Hill the views then and now are spectacular. One view was eastward over the miles of squares and oblongs of fields, shapes emphasised in the snow, and the orchards and woods to Gloucester, with its white cathedral tower, mass of grey houses and black needle-like church spires. Another was down over the Severn, like a colossal silver eel shining and twisting, to the blue Cotswolds, and another was westward over the Forest, less coniferous than today, into Wales. The place name of the view point, Double View, scarcely does justice to the panorama.

The journey to Gloucester in the spring, or to the neighbouring Pope's Hill, passed through two miles of whiteness—the blossom of thousands of plum, apple and pear trees. Pope's Hill is an area of smallholdings, in those days often of iron or coal miners. For them the sale of fruit and a few sheep supplemented the household income and the chicken and Gloucester Old Spot pigs provided eggs and bacon. The land is hilly and sandy, bracken and heather grow on the common land—good indicators of well drained, acidic soils. Victoria, Blaisdon Reds and several other local varieties of plums were grown and the apples were mainly cider apples.

'The magic names remain,
those old apples of cidered Gloucestershire,
Skyrmes Kernel, Dymock Red and Forest Styre,
Black Foxwhelps and Redstreak;
such honeyed sounds,
pure English poetry in my country ears'

Clark writes in his poem 'From Cider House'.

In spring the distinctive sound was the hum of bees on the fruit blossom, in autumn the sober drumming of the cider mill engine. Pope's Hill in blossom time was a special place for Clark [fig. 67].

The woods below the Forest rim, Chestnuts Inclosure to the north and Abbot's Wood to the south, were also special. Chestnuts Wood [fig. 68], looking like a 'giant's umbrella' when seen from Littledean Hill, was planted in 1812, as was much of the old oak woodland of the Forest of Dean [fig. 69]. Here Spanish chestnuts were included in the planting and a rich ground flora of bluebells and foxgloves flourished. Heart rot caused the felling of most trees in 1940 and Clark writes sadly of 'their magnificence and their ruin'. The replanting in 1949 introduced conifers and so contributed to a more limited wildlife, but badger and fox remained and so did the ruddled sheep. Abbot's Wood, from which in medieval times the monks had drawn their wood for the iron furnace at Flaxley, was also an oak-beech wood and then later used as an experimental area for various exotic trees, so giving it a patchwork appearance. Clark explored both woods as a child and he knew

69. MATURE OAK WOODLAND IN THE FOREST OF DEAN

their beauty with the changing seasons [fig. 70] and here too he would go in his teens to quietly write poetry.

Another place with an atmosphere for writing poetry was the Severn, 'the dazzling Severn', at Newnham. The mixture of surprise and excitement at the first sight of water from Newnham High Street was well remembered. The stretch of sand and the treacherous tide, the red sandstone cliffs with their grey bands and the church perched on top, the rotting boats along the shore, the elver and salmon fishers and above all the bore, gave to Newnham its particular character.

The four mile walk from his home to Newnham took him down the steep hill to Littledean, passing a stone quarry on the way. This was another place of early exploration. It was a roadstone quarry in the dolomite, where stone was cracked by hammer and then carried out by carts drawn by horses, or by traction engines. There were both tiered and tunnelled workings. Further north along the Forest edge were the Edge Hill iron mines in the Crease limestone, but by the 1910s these had long since ceased production and the miners had moved to the coal pits to the west. The old roads also attracted his interest. Packhorse roads once used to transport iron ore, an old pedlars track and the Dean road, a Roman road from Lydney to Ariconium, are mentioned. The section of this latter road at Blackpool Bridge, with its large sets, was the best known Roman road but there were others through Abbot's Wood and at the Ruffit.

Like so many children in the Forest of Dean at that time and since, Clark was encouraged in his music making. He played the church organ at St Stephen's and the piano for the cricket club sing song at the George at Littledean. He sang in the Cinderford Male Voice

70. A FOREST PATH INVITING EXPLORATION

Choir and enjoyed listening to the 'clouds of praise rolling over Cinderford from sixty voices in the Baptist chapel'. This is how he describes the scene in Gloucester Cathedral as he waited for the opening chords of the 'Messiah'.

> The Cathedral was packed, with a subdued rustle of conversation still going on. I looked round in gratitude. I smelt that peculiar must of the ages which old cathedrals have. Shafts of broken sunlight streamed through the windows like prayers flashing from heaven. One patch of red mingled with purple falling on a memorial tablet near by fascinated me for the whole of the service. The history of my county was written around me on wall and marble tomb. The dead city fathers slept on in their carved urns in sure and certain hope that in their flesh they would see God.

His childhood was poor in material terms but rich in scope for the imagination, geographically insular but unrestricted in the wanderings of the mind. He looks back on it with genuine gratitude. A treasured early Christmas gift was the *Oxford Book of Verse* and Clark makes use of his literary allusions with a light touch. These are never ostentatious. Thus he says his mother knew how to 'enjoy the world aright' and showed him the way to do so himself. To walk with her was to 'perceive the soul of beauty', a sentiment Laurie Lee would have appreciated. Or, like Edward Thomas on the other side of the county at Adlestrop, he writes from Littledean Hill 'over us all floated the white clouds of Gloucestershire with such a concentration of song beneath them as to suggest that every other county in England was birdless'. He writes of a world long gone but which went later from the Forest of Dean than from most parts of the country.

Other writers have described their childhood and early life in the Forest. Winifred Foley, a miner's daughter at Brierley Hill; Dennis Potter, a miner's son at Christ Church; George Aston, son of a crown woodman working in East Dean, have done so. But Leonard Clark was the first, and wrote from a more distant and reflective perspective, having moved away from the area some forty years previously. There is a strong theme of gratitude for his Forest upbringing in all his writings and also a sense of wonder that he expresses especially in his poems. So the collection 'The Way it was' ends with these lines of prayer:

> Keep a sense of wonder in me,
> an innocence that is not deceived or destroyed;
> then I can continue to see perfect images of you
> in all your creations,
> marvel at their glory and beauty,
> and so worship you better,
> Who are Perfection,
> from Everlasting to Everlasting.

A child-like innocence characterises his descriptions of the landscape and, in contrast to most other writers, he does not normally use pseudonyms for the local people he introduces to us in his books. He does not need to.

Places to visit: Cinderford for its Victorian housing, St Stephen's Church, and the miner's statue. Linear Park below Cinderford for a sense of the boundary between industry and forestry. Mature oak woodland, as Abbot's Wood. Littledean Hill for the views. Newnham for the Severn shore.

Laurie Lee

The Colourful Wordsmith of Slad

Cider with Rosie, 1959

Growing up in a female dominated household, poor and lacking much contact with the outside world, Laurie Lee graphically describes his boyhood response to the sensory stimuli around him in the Slad valley as he recalls his childhood there at the end of the First World War. *Cider with Rosie* has made the Slad valley the most famous of all Cotswold valleys and it is with the physical setting of the book that we are concerned in this chapter.

The Slad Brook is one of several that flow southward to the Frome near Stroud. The valley is steep-sided, with cattle pasture on the lower slopes and ridges crowned with beech woods framing it. It can be a funnel for winds and also a sun trap. Lee fondly describes it as a 'jungly, bird-crammed, insect-hopping sun trap whenever there happened to be any sun'. Sunshine was always important for him. Slad village [fig. 71] was then a loose cluster of twenty to thirty houses on the south east facing side. It was 'like living in a bean pod'. Some of the beech woods are now conservation areas, cattle and sheep still

71. SLAD VILLAGE

72. LAURIE LEE'S
CHILDHOOD HOME

graze the slopes as they have done for centuries but there are many more houses than there were when Lee described it and the B4070 running through the village is a busy road. Nevertheless the valley and its features are easily recognisable from the book.

His childhood home, Bank Cottages [fig. 72] (later Rosebank), was one of three stone cottages joined in a 'T' shape. It was one of the oldest houses in the village, dating from the seventeenth century, and like many similar Cotswold properties had once been a beer house. The rent was 3s 6d (18p) a week. Its walls were thick, keeping the damp chill in, its hand-carved mullion windows were full of plants screening the light, its interior was whitewashed and upstairs the ceilings were of varnished matchboarding. As it was built below a steep bank, there was always a risk of rain water running off the road and flooding the kitchen and cellar, otherwise water was pumped from a well.

At the bottom of the valley, by a lake, was the squire's house, Steanbridge, a sixteenth-century clothier's house with Georgian façade. After the squire's death it was sold by auction and became successively a nursing home, guest house and then again a private residence. There were several substantial farmhouses in the valley but even the vicarage was no larger than the boarding houses at Weston-super-Mare, observed on a memorable choir outing. Sometimes on the death of an elderly resident the more isolated cottages, such as those deep in the woods, were abandoned and soon became derelict. A few garden plants eventually became the only signs of their former existence.

In common with most old cottages, at Bank Cottage there was a large garden which was important for feeding the family. Crops of potatoes, peas, beans, carrots, strawberries, radishes and chives were grown but there was also space for the traditional cottage garden flowers, forget-me-nots, pansies, hollyhocks, foxgloves, poppies and pinks and also for roses growing into the apple trees, lilac, laburnum and flowering red currant. The squire's garden on the other hand had its lawns, cedars and main drive through beech trees.

Garden produce was supplemented by food gathered from the woods and hedgerows. From the woods Lee mentions damsons, sloes and crab apples—these were most likely

73. AN OLD CIDER APPLE
ORCHARD AT SLAD

from the woodland edges and hedgerows. From the Scrubs, then a waste area towards Bisley, came blackberries and hazelnuts and from the woods, gardens and meadows came the raw materials for homemade wines. The title of the book suggests cider orchards, and many farms in these milder western Cotswold valleys had a few apple trees for cider-making, though, as noted before, cider was not a typical Cotswold drink [fig. 73].

In those days before intensive farming, the meadows still yielded a wide range of wild flowers, which his mother picked for display in the cottage, and he notes there were rare orchids growing locally. The steep grassy slope of Swift's Hill [fig. 74], on the opposite side of the valley to his home, is now an important nature reserve where the orchids [fig. 75] and grasses and their attendant butterflies and bees are protected.

All the farmers kept horses, the principal source of power to work farm machinery and to pull the various carts, and most had cows. Lee vividly describes the winter stall

74. SWIFT'S HILL LOOKING TOWARDS STROUD

75. EARLY PURPLE ORCHID ON SWIFT'S HILL

feeding of the dairy cattle. 'Inside the cow sheds it was warm and voluptuous, smelling sweetly of milky breath, of heaving hides, green dung, and udders, of steam and fermentations. We carried cut hay from the heart of the rick, packed tight as tobacco flake, with grass and wild flowers juicily fossilized within—a whole summer embalmed in our arms'. The need to provide this essential winter feed explains the importance of haymaking. So grass grew taller then than the present day silage cutting allows and some of the originality of the book is derived from its frequent grass level perspectives from the time when, at the age of three, he was set down in it 'amongst grasshoppers leaping like monkeys' to the time when he lay in the grass with his young girlfriends—the grass of glow worms, sky larks' eggs and September mushrooms.

Villages were much more isolated and self-contained in those days, 'like ships in empty landscapes', and even when cut off by snow drifts in winter, the villagers coped. Slad possessed its shop and post office and pub, bread and milk were delivered daily and the fishmonger called weekly. It was in a large parish which included Sheepscombe as well as the main settlement of Painswick, where the rates were paid. Most people walked or cycled to shop in Stroud and the transport of bulky goods was by carrier's cart. The first choir outing Lee remembers was to Gloucester with transport by a farmer's wagon. By-roads were white, untarred, rutted and little used. The range of horse-drawn vehicles controlled the distances people usually travelled, with a twice weekly wagonette to Stroud and a daily carrier cart from Sheepscombe. Significant changes in transport did not occur here until the 1920s, first with a rare, brass-lamped car, then with the charabanc (five of these were needed for the choir outing to Weston) and then the solid tyred open top bus, at first weekly, then daily. Improved transport changed the employment opportunities for local people. No longer was there a need for young men to emigrate to the colonies, or young women to go away into domestic service, nor was nearby work confined to farms, or the cloth mills of the Stroud valley, or employment by the squire. And now the 'jazzy' shops of Gloucester were easily accessible.

Actually the oldest routeway in the village is the sunken track from Catswood to Bulls Cross, which crosses the Slad Brook at Steanbridge, near the pond where a villager drowned. This was a section of the early road from Cirencester to Gloucester, first recorded in 1353. The Stroud to Cheltenham road was not built until 1800.

76. PAINSWICK VIEWED
FROM BULL'S CROSS

There was a social hierarchy in the village as seen both in the church seating pattern and in the strategic planning of the annual carol singing route, with squire followed by doctor, merchant, major and farmers. But as the latter was a five mile round trip it may have incorporated other settlements. Slad was a squire village and the squire still took some responsibility for caring for the needy. He opened his grounds for days of celebration and provided employment and social leadership. Unusually for a squire village there was also a chapel and manse, but as Lee sang in the church choir the chapel does not figure prominently in his boyhood memory. Church attendance, particularly on Sunday mornings, was almost complete for the village and the important festivals brought the whole community together. Harvest Festival was the most popular; 'to enter the church on Harvest morning was like crawling head first into a horn of plenty, a bursting granary, a vegetable stall, a grotto of bright flowers'. The range of social contacts was limited but contacts were much more frequent than today and villagers were interdependent.

Occasionally Lee gives a startling description of a nearby place. Painswick, viewed from Bull's Cross, was sprawling white 'like the skeleton of a foundered mammoth' [fig. 76], or at night 'a starfish of light'. Bull's Cross was 'a baldness among the woods, a ragged wildness of bent turves'. It is still common land, where the tracks and former stage-coach roads cross, and where orchids and helleborines grow. Deadcombe Bottom was a gloom of dank, yellow wood, where around an abandonned cottage it was 'silent, birdless and sunless'.

Many visitors writing on the Cotswold landscape emphasize the contrast between spring, with its fresh new life, and autumn, with the copper tints of the beech woods, but for Lee the chief contrast was between summer and winter. Winter was cold, with frost patterns on the windows, trees coated with ice, springs like frozen flowers. It was marked by the death of small birds, crows worrying the sheep, snow drifts up to the hedges and conditions especially hard for the elderly. 'It was a world of glass, sparkling and motionless. Vapours had frozen all over the trees and transformed them into confections of sugar. Everything was rigid, locked-up and sealed, and when we breathed the air it smelt like needles and stabbed our nostrils and made us sneeze', true 'Cotswold cold'. Hot summer brought the smell of burnt sap and roast nettles and the calls of the cuckoo and wood pigeon, the grass was 'June high and had come up with a rush, a massed entanglement of species, crested with flowers and spears of wild wheat, and coiled with clambering vetches, the whole of it humming with blundering bees and flickering with scarlet butterflies'.

Smells and sounds seemed at times more significant to him than colours and textures. In autumn gales 'the woods roared night and day stiring great seas of sound' but it could also be a world of silence, when the call of the owl could be heard far away, or the creaking of wagon and jingle of harness as a farm cart passed. The quality of light also drew his attention, from the dim interior of the cottage, to the evening glow on the opposite fields with cows 'brilliant as painted china'. His observations and his writings both possess a feminine sensitivity.

As with his later books Lee relied on his diaries to recall the sensations of his earlier years, but in writing *Cider with Rosie* he was helped by letters his mother sent him, and parts of the book originated in magazine pieces which were published from 1941 onwards. These were favourably received and he was encouraged to write more, but even so the expected sales of the complete book were no more than 800 copies. In fact over a million paperback copies had been sold by 1977 following its selection as a school text. He had written poems, plays and film scripts before, but this autobiographical account of a rural childhood in the Cotswolds, described in such lush prose, attracted widespread attention. He was largely self-taught as a writer and from early in his writing career had worked on similes and word pictures so that, although some felt his descriptions were overdone and too packed with imagery, all could appreciate the sharpness of his eye and the sensitivity of his observations. And although it is a very local book, it resonates with rural childhood everywhere in England at this time. As a result the Slad valley became a tourist destination with its inn, the Woolpack, as its focus.

The book is illustrated by fine line drawings by John Ward, a *Vogue* artist, who understood the countryside well and empathised with Lee's writing.

This then was the setting for Lee's early life, of the fears, fevers and frolics he describes, a place of muddle, music and mortality, a place that by the time of the book's completion in 1959, had already become, he says, a home of pensioners. He courageously moved back to Slad at this time and faced some of the disquiet of family and neighbours about the disclosures in his memoirs and also a libel action for one of its observations. From then on Slad became his country base until his death in 1997, and largely through his influence during those years the valley has not been 'developed' by the threatened expansion of Stroud. He was buried beside the steep path to the church, which he had so often walked as a boy seventy years before. 'He lies in the valley he loved' is engraved upon his tombstone.

Places to visit: Rosebank, his childhood home, lies just below the B4070, NE of the church. The Woolpack. The church, where he was a choirboy—his grave is by the upper church path. The school is now a private house. Bull's Cross, with views of Painswick and the starting point of many country walks. Swift's Hill for a good view of Slad and for its old grassland, once typical of so many Cotswold pastures. His later home was Rose Cottage behind the Woolpack. The Laurie Lee cricket ground is at Sheepscombe.

John Moore

A Naturalist with Roots in Tewkesbury

A Portrait of Elmbury, 1946

This was the first of three autobiographical novels written by John Moore. It describes aspects of his life in and around Tewkesbury up to the time of the Second World War. Although the names of people and places have been changed and some details of the geography of the area have been altered, so that for example one could not follow some of the journeys he describes, the book conveys the atmosphere of Tewkesbury in the 1920s and 1930s with sympathy, understanding and affection.

Moore was born into an old, established, professional, Tewkesbury family. His early home was Tudor House [fig. 77], through whose leaded windows he observed with fascination the life of the High Street and its feeder alleys. Preparatory school at Colwell introduced him to natural history, through a revered classics master. Here he began his collection of butterflies and moths and an interest in the local birds, mammals and fish as he was encouraged to explore the area. He became in time an outstanding naturalist. His years at Malvern College were unfulfilling, but avid and undiscriminating reading must have contributed to the quality of his own later writing. At seventeen he joined the respectable family firm of estate agents and this brought him into contact with people from all walks of life and especially with the farming community. Market days and farm sales were major social events for the farmers. So he was able to write with genuine concern of the outbreak of foot and mouth disease in 1923, and of the damaging effect of a late frost to the fruit growers at Bredon, and of the despair caused by the 1930s depression. It was, however, the sadness of having to conduct the sale of a poor debtor's furniture that finally moved him to leave the firm and become a writer. He became a newspaper correspondent during the Spanish Civil War, a pilot in the Fleet Air Arm in the Second World War, and then, for twenty years, columnist for countryside matters for the Birmingham *Evening Mail*. In addition to the Brensham trilogy, consisting of *A Portrait of Elmbury*, *Brensham Village* and *The Blue Field*, he wrote many novels and books on the local area, some forty in all. In his later years he lived at Lower Mill, Kemerton. He died in 1967 at the age of 59 and is buried by the south wall of the Abbey.

77. TUDOR HOUSE,
MOORE'S CHILDHOOD
HOME

Tudor House is one of three dozen sixteenth-century, timber-framed buildings that survive in Tewkesbury. Some buildings are older. The fashion of timber framing with mud and wattle infill ended at about 1700, and in the following Georgian period houses were brick built. The three main streets of the town, High Street, Church Street and Barton Street, contain good examples of these too. Moore notes the pinkish-orange Georgian brickwork of the walls, which have an almost incandescent glow in strong sunlight. There are also the imitation styles of the nineteenth century, leading on to some standardised, insensitive and intrusive buildings of the late twentieth century. Tudor House draws on all except the latest of these fashions. It has a brick frontage with rainwater heads dated 1701, mock Tudor false timbers were added in 1897, its restored stone gateway is late seventeenth century and within the side garden is a lead cistern dated 1741. Moore calls it the loveliest house in Tewkesbury and Pevsner agrees about its interest.

Many of these sixteenth-century houses had side passages containing the main entrance to the house. The passages later gave access to other houses built in the back courts or alleys. The oak framework of the houses was generally of new timber which was soft and so when it was necessary to

78. A JETTIED SHOP AT THE END OF THE
HIGH STREET

cut the wood it could be done more easily. The timber has subsequently warped and twisted on drying out and ageing. Many houses are jettied [fig. 78]. Jetties gave more space on the upper floors, though the ground floor was the most important level of the house. The overhangs gave weather protection to the lower walls and the whole structure was stronger, and Alec Clifton-Taylor has suggested that the weight of the projecting wall counterbalanced the weight of heavy oak furniture, so preventing the sagging of the floors. Some of the brackets supporting the jetties and the spandrels of the doorways are very finely carved. Tewkesbury's limited prosperity in the major rebuilding periods checked the destruction of these old timbered properties and so contributed to their remarkable survival. When vertical frontages became more fashionable, many half-timbered houses were refronted and so extended towards the street, and in some cases plaster pargetting was applied to cover the timber framework. Moore likens these crooked, leaning houses to old wives gossiping. A few houses retain their leaded lights and in some cases with the original glass. Some Georgian properties also have their original handmade crown glass. This is thicker in the middle of the pane and so gives distortion to the view from the inside and to the reflection on the outside. The rich mixture of properties from the fifteenth to the eighteenth centuries provides Tewkesbury with its architectural charm [fig. 79], but one has to look above the shop windows and named fascia boards to appreciate this.

79. TEWKESBURY'S UNIQUE BLEND OF DIFFERENT MATERIALS AND STYLES OF BUILDING

Until the livestock market was established in the Oldbury in 1926, markets were held in the wide streets. According to sixteenth-century bye-laws the upper High Street, north of Quay Lane, was for cattle, the lower High Street for corn, Church Street for sheep and Barton Street for general tradesmen—hatters, coopers, tanners etc. The Cross, where the Toll Booth or Tolsey also stood, was the focal point of the market. At several places these generally wide streets are narrower and at one time the constrictions were much more severe with their clutter of buildings. The entry into the High Street from Church Street was eight feet wide and into Barton Street even less, and at the south end of Church Street there were five more properties extending Abbey Cottages to within a few feet of the Bell Inn. Widening took place here in 1786.

Narrower still were the alleys and courts [fig. 80]. There were about a

80. MAP OF
HIGH STREET,
TEWKESBURY
AT THE TIME
OF MOORE'S
CHILDHOOD

hundred alleys crammed with substandard housing and with a dense population. Moore refers to their filth, squalor and nauseous condition. As a child he could watch events in the most notorious of the alleys, Double Alley, from his window in Tudor House. He thought that as slums they were far worse than those of the East End of London. The entrance to Double Alley is described as the gaping jaws of a medieval hell. In the language of an official report the houses were 'exceedingly filthy and unwholesome'. Two hundred of the hovels had no privies according to an 1849 survey and they were undrained. The alleys originally led to the workshops, stores and gardens of the properties facing the street, but the later rows of cottages were built to provide rent for the landholders. Some alley properties, such as those of Baptist Court, were of the sixteenth century, others as in Double Alley were older, but most were built in the late seventeenth and eighteenth centuries. In the 1841 census Double Alley had twenty-nine houses and a population of 100. TB, cholera and smallpox outbreaks were common. Moore writes of the ragged women, drunken men, screaming wanton wenches and naked rickety children living in the worst of the alleys. Double Alley was cleared in 1944, but the slum clearance was not always popular with the residents because removal inevitably meant higher rents, less accessible amenities and community breakup. The alleys on the east side of the upper High Street bend as they approach the street. This is because their main alignment follows that of the strips of the former Oldbury open field. These were at an acute angle to the High Street, so the alleys bend to become normal to the High Street as they run between the frontage properties.

There were many pubs in Tewkesbury, thirty-five premises were licenced in 1891 and Moore says there were twenty-eight in his youth. The names and status of the inns, pubs and hotels have frequently changed and relatively few remain today. The livestock market was an important factor in their prosperity. The Swan had the bar for the farmers and the Shakespeare for farmers' sons. Business often continued in the Red Lion, which was also the drovers' pub. When the market closed in the 1960s these all lost trade. At an earlier date the coaching inns prospered. These were the Swan in the High Street, the Royal Hop Pole in Church Street and the Star and Garter in Barton Street. The George, noted for its drunken fights, was the local for the alley dwellers. Each hostelry had its own character, atmosphere and clientele and Moore obtained much information about the life of the town from the heterogeneous group that regularly met at the Swan, as he did later at the Fox and Hounds at Bredon.

With a population of about 5000 in the 1920s, Tewkesbury began to attract the attention of the chain stores. These acquired the larger properties and slowly began to squeeze out the small family businesses. Moore was well aware of this trend and disliked it, as indeed he did all tyrannous big businesses. He comments on the loss of two or three old family businesses with each new arrival and appreciated the humour of one trader who was suffering from the competition of a store with the motto *mens sana in corpore sano* and who responded with the superior version of *mens and womens sana in corpore sano*!

Moore summarises the main industries in Tewkesbury in the early twentieth century as flour milling, malting and boat building. He also hints at decline, quoting as evidence a disused flour mill, ruined warehousing and derelict shirt and mustard factories. Flour milling has a long history here with the Abbey Mill and then the Borough Mill, the former was water-powered and the latter originally steam-powered, but both relied on the river to transport grain. Malting too was an old industry and although declining by the early nineteenth century, continued into the twentieth with the Abbey Brewery in Smith Lane, the Town Brewery in Quay Street and a malthouse in Sheep Street. In the nineteenth century the largest employment was in textiles, especially in cotton hosiery knitting, and several buildings used in this way survive today. The derelict shirt factory was in Post Office Lane on a site formerly occupied by the Eagle Shoe Factory and before this by a tannery. No certain location of mustard making is known and reference to Tewkesbury mustard after the time of Shakespeare is always vague. Boat building at Bathursts' Boat Yard, north of St John's Bridge, is now continued at the large leisure boat marina.

Most of the town's population was dependent on agriculture, not only in farm work, or directly supplying or supporting the farming community as dealers in hay, corn, or cattle, auctioneers and implement suppliers, but also in retailing generally associated with it. So when agriculture was depressed the whole town economy suffered. In 1932 it was estimated that 31% of the working population was unemployed. Then, in particular, the odd job men could find little work. The odd job man with his independence, initiative, inventiveness and range of skills was well able to support his family in normal times. His was a lifestyle that gave freedom and variety, and was not without its financial success, as the following account of a 1925 income shows. 'From casual work on farms such as sprout picking, plum picking, haymaking, harvesting, rick cutting, droving and rabbiting 31%, from fishing for salmon and eels 17%, from other river work on barges, osier cutting, sand dredging and punt repairs 19%, from country sports, gillying for fishermen, beating for shoots, earth stopping for the hunt 8%, from sale of produce from the allotment including a pig 9%, from timber cutting 5% and from picking mushrooms and blackberries 4%.' Apart from poaching and other illegal activities the total income was twice that of a farm labourer and for a flexible four day week!

Tewkesbury is surrounded by land liable to flood. To the west between the Severn and Avon is Severn Ham, which is often flooded in the winter and has its fertility maintained by the deposits of silt from the water. In common with other hams near towns, it had a complex pattern of ownership and hay crops and grazing rights were held by different people. So, for example, a seventeenth-century ruling gave grazing rights to the freeholders and burgesses of Tewkesbury. These were usually the people who owned properties on the main streets. Grazing was permitted after haymaking from Lammas (1st August) to Candlemas (2nd February) and each freeholder was allowed grazing for three horses, six cows or ten sheep. Severn Ham was also a leisure area for Tewkesbury people for walks, cricket and horse racing. For Moore its main attraction was its bird life of curlew, redshank, snipe and lapwing and, in winter months, ducks and geese and also its fishing banks, where not only salmon and eels could be caught, but also the river fish—chubb, roach, bream, bleak, perch and minnows.

His old prep school master had fostered an early interest in butterflies and moths and the master's collection of such colourful specimens as swallow tails, Kentish glory, red underwing and many hawk moths, inspired Moore to make his own collection. This was later presented to the Gloucester City Museum. He mentions the especially exciting discovery of a convolvulus hawk moth on a tree trunk in a larch plantation on Bredon Hill. This was a rare visitor from the continent, or possibly from Africa. H.A. Evans in his book on Gloucestershire estimated that there were between seven and eight hundred species of butterflies and moths in the county in the 1920s. But habitat destruction and more intensive farming methods have sadly contributed to diminished numbers, both of species and individuals. Moore mentions the value of such garden flowers as penstemon, tobacco and valerian to attract moths.

In the Portrait of Elmbury, other birds beside those of the river are referred to, linnets, larks and goldfinches on Brockeridge Common, magpies and hawks in the woods on Bredon Hill, long-tailed tits nesting in the sloe bushes at its foot, nightingales in the hazel hedge along Gander Lane, little owls newly arrived in the county but fairly widespread by the 1920s and whitethroats nesting among stinging nettles. Fewer wild animals are included but there is a discussion on the role of foxhunting in the countryside. The hunt met on Boxing Day at the Swan and Moore rode with the hounds in his younger days. However, he had reservations about it. He thought hunting served to keep down the numbers of foxes but also to preserve them. It created employment, but most of this was unproductive, it was democratic in the sense that the hunt and followers went on all kinds of private property and if a landowner opposed this free access there were strong social sanctions against him. It taught lessons about the countryside that the riders would not have otherwise learned.

Moore recognised the role of hedgerows in giving texture to the landscape and records the species growing in one example—hazel, hawthorn, elm, sloe, elder and spindle, two of which, hazel and spindle, suggest it was an old one. He responds to the poetry of field and wood names as seen in farm sales catalogues, although the one example he gives, Starveal, is rather inauspicious.

Being a market town with its banks and shops, Tewkesbury was a central place for the surrounding villages. It did not match the industrial prosperity of Gloucester, or the social prosperity of Cheltenham, but it served its neighbourhood well. Moore observed that there were about twelve villages dependent on Tewkesbury, twice the number one would normally expect. He distinguished each settlement by its sporting prowess, its principal occupations, or by the reputed character of its inhabitants! But each was a social entity gathered around church, pub, shop and village hall. The only exception to this pattern was a 'squire village', where dependency on the squire had made it, in Moore's view, a sterilized place, lacking in individuality. The bridge points of the rivers, the barrier of Bredon Hill and the nearness of the county boundary probably have some bearing on Tewkesbury's catchment area.

81. TEWKESBURY ABBEY DURING WINTER FLOODS

The abbey, old houses and river attracted tourists from much further afield. Some were Birmingham day-trippers coming by the coachload, for whom cafes and tea rooms were opened, shops sold souvenirs and trivia, and boat trips were provided on the river. Others, including Americans, would stay in one of the hotels of the town. Tudor House with its twelve bedrooms became a hotel in 1918, on the death of Moore's father. The Royal Hop Pole advertised its Dickens link and the Bell its ancient bowling green. Moore mentions the Italian tea rooms near the Abbey of Palmiro Barsanti. In the nineteenth century, as with so many towns, there had been an attempt to develop a spa along the Ashchurch Road. The Abbey, Moore thought, has the finest Norman tower in the world [fig. 81] and this dominates the town, rising above the chestnut, cedar and mulberry trees of the churchyard. It was part of the town and had, he says, no odour of sanctity about it. But apart from the controversial open air plays to raise money for its upkeep, he writes little about it.

The character of Tewkesbury itself is the subject of the book, with its incomparable beauty and incomparable squalor and ugliness, both splendid and sordid, higgledy-piggledy, rather like the varied lives and outlooks of the people who lived there. The pen portraits of his prep school master, the old colonel with his shooting and fishing exploits, the prim bar maid at the Swan and the staid farmers and their reckless sons are drawn with warmth and affection. They are valued as individuals.

Although the names of people are ficticious, the views they express are true to life. Farmers do like to be known at market, they don't fish, they do marry farmers daughters and for many of them it pays best to buy best. Similarly Moore understood the countryside well with its sights and sounds and smells. He writes of the poet 'he sees things more sharply than we do and matches his words to what he sees'. In this sense Moore was a poet. From his school days when he read poetry 'like a sea lion swallowing fish' and his time in the estate agent's office with 'its vocabulary rich in nouns and more beggarly range of adjectives', he developed a style of writing that was relaxed, generous and often spiced with humour. His description of Tirley 'all mists and miasmas', of the 'pink flamingo clouds' above the Abbey tower on a summer evening, of the robin from the back looking like a 'round shouldered, disillusioned businessman wearing a brown mackintosh too big for him', and of the rivers 'tying Tewkesbury into an untidy parcel', are typical.

He distrusted the role of government and of suburban views in country matters. He was opposed to the power of big business, whether in the form of chain stores or shooting syndicates. He campaigned against the use of chemical sprays and later in life set up a conservation area at Kemerton. But he will be best remembered for his insight into the changing countryside in the twentieth century and locally by the little museum in the Abbey Cottages that bears his name. His view is that of a naturalist with a genuine feel for country life.

Places to visit: Tudor House Hotel, John Moore Countryside Museum, the Abbey, Severn Ham. Take a leisurely walk along Tewkesbury's main streets to observe the buildings on the opposite side of the road.

C. Henry Warren

The Rural Economy of the Inter-War Period on the Cotswold Edge

A Cotswold Year, 1936

Where there was no main road joining together the spring-line settlements at the foot of the Cotswold escarpment, their relative inaccessibility led to small independent rather introspective communities. The less favourable farming conditions here meant that these communities were poorer than many others in the weak economy of the mid-1930s. During the years 1932–1936, the writer C. Henry Warren came to rent a house at Stockend (Woodend in the book) and, as he says, to watch the slow procession of the seasons and share in the quiet lives and activities of the country folk.

Stockend nestles in one of the many embayments of the Cotswold scarp face [fig. 82]. These are usually called combes (from the Anglo-Saxon 'cumb', meaning a short valley), Harescombe in this case. The higher slopes are thickly wooded and limestone quarries have been cut into their upper rim. Beneath the steep beech woods the pasture land slopes less steeply down to Daniel's Brook and so on to the Severn, that 'twists like a silver serpent through the trees', the trees then being mainly elms. Robinswood Hill hides Gloucester Cathedral from view but the southern outskirts of the city were seen with their red roofs, factories, gasometers, airfield and slums and beyond were the Malverns 'like a crouching lion'. To the extreme left is May Hill and Warren mentions the crest of bracken shining there in the autumn sunlight but strangely omits the conspicuous clump of pine trees that crowns the hill. The main view is north-westwards [fig. 83] but the only lane access to Stockend is from Edge, so all external links are eastwards on to the Cotswolds.

Warren understood the changes taking place at the time, even in this isolated community. He recognised that the new bus service, which gave access to shops in towns like Stroud and Gloucester, reduced the dependence of the village on the local store—a development which later continued with car ownership and affected not only the village store but also all the village services. The cohesion that shop, school and post office gave to the rural communities was thereby weakened, although there was ample opportunity for sociability on the bus. The private car also enabled 'townies' to live for the first time in the countryside at a distance from railway stations and so the first signs of property

82. THE SETTING
OF STOCKEND

conversions were to be seen in rural areas, here with the alteration of the water mill into a very desirable residence. He records that a petrol pump had just been introduced into the carefully restored seventeenth-century ambience of Stanton and concludes that, with the decline in the number of farm and carriers' horses, the days of the wheelwright and blacksmith were numbered. Declining employment opportunities in the country led to rural depopulation and he could count four derelict houses in sight of his own cottage and others that were deteriorating through lack of maintenance.

Change was also occuring in the use of farmland. Cotswold fields, that for years had been sheep pastures and still retained their richly diverse flora, were being ploughed up for winter wheat as subsidised prices for the latter had risen. Some hedges were being replaced by fences, with space and drainage gains for cropland. But farming on the scarp face was noticeably less prosperous and less advanced than that of the Vale, where soils were deeper and grazing was lush.

83. THE VIEW
WEST FROM
STOCKEND

Other tell-tale signs of change were wireless aerials on every cottage. These brought up-to-date national news and London entertainment to the villages and so made the homespun variety a rather taudry affair. The pace of life was quickening in the thirties but the older residents were always ready to stop for a chat.

The book contains many deft and lively descriptions of traditional country work, of the loneliness of dry stone walling, of hedge laying, of haymaking when 'hay seeds cling to sweaty skin', of thatching, and of cider making, which gives to autumn its smell. Warren observes the daffodil pickers near Dymock, where the cost of entry to the fields for picking the flowers was between 1d and 3d depending on location, and the Welsh cattle drovers leaving Barton Fair in Gloucester and the elver fishermen in the evening along the Severn at the time of the high bores. From the natural world he listens with a musician's ear to the songs of blackbird, skylark and nightingale, he enjoys the spectacle of hares boxing and of rooks squabbling over nesting materials and the swarms of butterflies rising from hot sunny banks as he walks past. The striking colour combination of six spot burnets on scabious flowers catches his attention [fig. 84], as does the tar black trees following a May frost and the pinpricks of wild strawberries showing through the foliage. There are many memorable turns of phrase—'the sky the colour of grocer's sugar paper', appropriate before prepackaging, and 'sky larks held up by song'. But he saves his most evocative writing for the woods above his cottage, 'secretive from the outside, green within, even the air seems green' [fig. 85] and where there is the 'scarcely audible whisper of leaves rubbing against leaves, leaves growing, leaves dying'. Today the understorey of sycamore saplings beneath the mature beech trees and the ground flora of dog's mercury, garlic, ivy and ferns give further emphasis to this green colour.

Reference is made to some twenty people in the book—farmers and their wives, the shopkeeper, the post lady—ordinary people, country people, people with their roots in the area, people he values for their lack of artificial sophistication and for their sense of proportion. Although he finds them superstitious and prejudicial, he prefers this to the narrow subjectivism he sees in townspeople and the spiteful gossip of suburbia. But of course it takes more than four years to be fully integrated into a community such as this, especially with such an eccentric occupation as that of a writer. So his views are always those of an outsider looking in and he writes for a similar readership.

He is conscious of the social divisions in the villages,

84. SIX SPOT BURNETS ON SCABIOUS FLOWERS

85. THE GREEN ATMOSPHERE OF THE WOODS

perhaps best revealed in park palings, where the quietly sedate and leisured affluence within contrasts with the daily busyness of village life without. The two opposite views through the wrought iron and pillared gates convey a class distinction which Warren recognises. Another social distinction he mentions is with the colony at Whiteway, where the tin-roofed huts and scattered bungalows sat uneasily in the Cotswold landscape and where some of Tolstoy's ideals were still lived out.

He travelled to the notable places in the Cotswolds, to Broadway, with its 'cult of beauty', to Campden, less pampered but with a 'beauty used and loved in the using', to Painswick, 'prim, sombre and self-conscious'. He savours the eighteenth-century layout of Cirencester Park, the Roman mosaics at Chedworth, where he notes that the now inaccessible figure of summer has a twinkle in his eye, the stacked effigies of the Fettiplace family in Swinbrook church (a short distance east of Burford) and the homemade design of the tower of Sheepscombe church.

Farm implements he describes such as the tedder, tumbler and swath turner are no longer to be seen, apart from in museums, nor are cocks or ricks found today in the corners of fields. Farm museums are also the places to see the traditional farm wagon [fig. 86]. Warren describes one new example, fresh from the wheelwright's, with its crimson body and dished orange wheels. The traditional colours for Cotswold wagons were yellow for the body, venetian red for the undercarriage, with black iron work. In the Vale the wheels were broader to cope with the mud. Different types of wood were used for the wagon's parts, elm for wheel hubs and floor boards, oak for wheel spokes and body

86. COTSWOLD FARM WAGONS AT THE COUNTRYSIDE MUSEUM, NORTHLEACH

frame, beech for wheel rims and axles, ash for sides and ladders, each type of wood being chosen for its special properties. So the wheelwright's yard contained a wide variety of timber. The nearest wheelwright to Stockend was two villages away. There are few traces of wheelwrights today and most of their yards have been built over. But there are traces of blacksmiths' forges, for the name is almost invariably preserved in the present day converted property and a few blacksmiths still work in the area specialising in ornamental gates, weather vanes and house signs.

As he moves through the months of the year, Warren notes the weather patterns and, although as he says spring takes little heed of the calendar, there is sufficient detail in the book to identify differences from the weather of the present day. For example, the horse chestnut trees came into flower on 13th June, a month later than nowadays. Graphs of mean monthly temperatures for the 1930s and for today in Gloucestershire clearly show the differences. Snow fall is less today and was perceived to be declining in the thirties.

The farming year has changed too but not primarily because of the weather. New varieties of crops and more powerful and efficient machinery mean that new land can be cultivated and crops harvested at different times than in the past. Rarely is ploughing seen in January, nor are hot fields of stubble found in September. Winter muck-spreading has often been replaced by applications of chemical fertilizers as and when the crops need it. Silage making in May has displaced haymaking in June. And the late autumn picking of plums, pears and apples does not now make a significant contribution to farm income. But 'Penny Farm' which in the 1930s was too small for agricultural prosperity and like most farms lacked the capital for developing specialist enterprises, remains the same size, it is still grassland, 'thin pasture' Warren calls it, but now focusses on horse riding. Some adjacent farms are managed along environmental lines and others maintain large dairy herds and continue muck-spreading. Daniel's Brook is dammed for fishing lakes.

Warren's book expresses observations that are sharp and sympathetic. It records the perceptions of a well-travelled and educated man of a lifetime ago. It describes landscapes and life-styles which were changing and with the approach of the Second World War would change more rapidly over the next decade. Some of his observations may seem unnecessary, such as churchyard yews as guardians of our puritan inheritance, and others are of more general significance than to 'Woodend'. As a professional writer he seems always to be on the lookout for new material to write about, all is grist for his mill. So inevitably, without the perspective of time, some material is trivial and ephemeral but there is much of lasting value. Of special significance is his insight into to the felt upheaval in the countryside caused by the introduction of new technology in the years just before the Second World War. The importance of the book lies not so much in its observations of the changing seasons seen in the Cotswold year, as the title suggests, but in its descriptions of the changes occurring in these years of his Cotswold residence. Warren was born near Maidstone in Kent in 1895 and after a brief period of teaching lived mainly by writing. This was supplemented by work for the BBC and he gave several broadcast talks on the Cotswolds. After leaving Stockend he moved to Finchingfield in Essex, where he continued to write on country matters and where he died in 1966. *A Cotswold Year* is a good example of his writing.

Places to visit: The best way to appreciate the setting of the book is to walk from Edge along the lane to Stockend and to follow the waymarked path to the Haresfield lane and then turning up hill to return along the bridleway through the woods above the settlement. Allenhay was his home at Stockend.

H.J. Massingham

An Informed Analyst of the Cotswold Landscape

Cotswold Country, 1937

Cotswold Country was H.J. Massingham's second contribution to the Batsford series *The Face of Britain*, published just before the Second World War and issued again during the war. Massingham was a perceptive and informed observer of the countryside and wrote of his personal responses to what he saw with telling metaphor and simile, so stimulating reflection on the part of his readers. He knew the area well and had lived for a while at Blockley. He thought that intimacy was more significant than specialist knowledge for such writing. The book is an account of a journey over the limestone from the cliffs at Burton Bradstock in Dorset to the low hills of Lincolnshire. But the bulk is concerned with the Gloucestershire Cotswolds where the Oolite outcrop is widest.

His dominant theme is limestone and the control it exercises over the landscape. Regional geography in Britain at the time followed the French school by exploring the concept of 'pays'. A pays is an integrated landscape in which the component elements are bonded together by some dominant influence, which could be climate, geology, relief, soil type, vegetation, or occasionally some human variable. This control was exerted over agriculture, house type, settlement pattern and economic opportunities and the task for the human geographer was to unravel these man/land relationships. The subtleties of these relationships were often expressed in art form, in the regional novel, music and landscape painting. Sometimes there seems to be an almost teleological sense, as if the control element had some inherent property that determined how the landscape developed, and Massingham comes close to this view when he writes of the continuity of craftsmanship in stone, 'Some deep spring of inspiration might well reside within this stone, since through it such power of creation has been kindled in the human spirit and has burned undimmed from age to age'.

Oolite takes its name from the small spherical particles, like fish roe, that make up the stone. Each particle has a fragment of shell or a grain of sand in the centre and this is surrounded by thin concentric layers of calcium carbonate. The conditions of salinity and temperature in which calcium carbonate can be precipitated and the turbulence in which

87. OOLITE EXPOSURE AT LECKHAMPTON HILL.
NOTICE THE SLOPE ANGLE CORRESPONDS TO
THE SCREE ANGLE

successive layers can be added are those of a shallow tropical or subtropical sea. The relative purity of the rock indicates a sea bordered by desert lands from which little sediment has been brought by rivers. The sizes of the spheres vary. Usually they are of pinhead size but they can be much larger, as with the pea grit at Crickley Hill. Some layers of the rock contain fossils of shells and so give the rough ragstone often used in drystone walls, but much is fossil free. This is the 'free stone', which has provided the best Cotswold building stone [fig. 87]. There are two main beds of Oolite, Great and Inferior, separated by a thin clayey layer of Fuller's Earth. There are no significant differences between these two beds, their joint patterns and composition are similar, but Massingham thought that the Inferior Oolite was the darker of the two.

He was more concerned with the colour of the stone than any other characteristic. There is not only the colour range from the silver-grey as at Painswick and Minchinhampton, through the buffs at the Guitings, to the 'autumnal tawniness' in the villages like Ebrington, north-east of Chipping Campden, which reveals the differences in the ferric carbonate content of the stone, but also the stone's property of being able to change tone with the weather. He writes that 'it reciprocates the moods of the day', and compares a street such as Chipping Campden's High Street to the changing expressions of a person's face. He attributes this characteristic to the way in which the stone reflects the yellow and violet components of the light spectrum. He also notices how the sharpness of the outlines of buildings with long roof ridges and angular gables is softened and veiled by the grey colouring and how the buildings seem to slip into the greenery under dark clouds and emerge again in the sunshine.

In his *Wold without End*, Massingham drew out the contrast between the north and south Cotswolds. The northern Cotswolds are true wolds, rounded, swelling, cloud country, while the southern Cotswolds are flatter and plateau-like. In *Cotswold Country* the contrast is made between the Edge and the Wold. The western Edge is higher and behind its scalloped cliff line are deeply incised, branching valleys—'bottoms' in the south, and more rounded bays—combes in the north. The abrupt landforms here contrast with the 'large calm benignity' of the Wolds to the east. This difference he attributes to the impact

88. SHERBORNE
HOUSE,
'ITALIANATE
CONFECTIONARY'

of the Lias clay of the Vale but it is more likely to be due to the greater erosive power of
the Severn tributaries, with their steeper gradient to the sea in contrast to the more gently
flowing tributaries of the upper Thames. The Severn–Thames watershed best marks the
division between the Edge and the Wold for most of the Cotswolds, with the upper reaches
of the Bristol Avon replacing the Thames in the extreme south of the region.

The traditional buildings of the Cotswolds are all of Oolite and their structural forms
are those best suited to the stone. From medieval times through to the Georgian period
and later, the Cotswold style is characterised by solid, simple, durable buildings. Although
earlier buildings were thatched, and thatch is still fairly common in the north-east of the
Cotswolds, from the seventeenth century roofs were of Stonesfield slate, with a simple
linear ridge and steep pitch. Massingham suggests that the pitch of 50–55 degrees allowed
for weathering, but the main reason was to enable the walls to better carry the heavy
weight of the roof. The roof space was used for rooms lit by dormer or gable windows in
the roof, or by windows in the gable ends. A steep pitch also meant that buildings were
narrow from front to back, typically less than eighteen feet, so the through rooms with
windows front and back could be lighter and better ventilated than rooms with a single
window. The basic plan was rectangular and could be extended into L-shaped, or even
courtyard houses.

Features seen in the medieval houses continued through the centuries, stone-framed
windows with mullions and transomes, arched doorways, drip stones, labels ('square
eyebrows' Massingham calls them) and hoodmoulds, and finials decorating gable tops.
Individual charm was given by fitments, ornaments, porches and windows of differing
sizes, and these varied with time and place. But the common style gave unity to groups
of buildings constructed over several centuries and ranging in scale from isolated farm,
dovecote and barn, through clusters in villages to town streets. Typically good examples are
the villages of Hampnett and Siddington and the High Street in Chipping Campden.

Some houses are given fuller descriptive comments in the book, manors such as
Owlpen, Upper Swell and Aston-sub-Edge, and Grevel's House, Chipping Campden,
houses appropriate in scale to their settings, courteous and discrete. Massingham does not
approve of the later pompous and overbearing country houses of Italianate confectionary,

89. SUMMER CROWDS AT BOURTON-ON-THE-WATER

so exhibitionist and arrogant. He particularly disliked it when the parish church was completely overshadowed, where the portentous and the meek stand side by side as at Chastleton, Sherborne [fig. 88] and Cowley. Nor, like other writers, does he approve of the invasion of blue slate, red brick and corrugated iron, which in the 1930s he says, was sprawling over all the geological formations of England, impervious to values and harmonies. So Bourton-on-the-Water [fig. 89] was castigated as the Wigan rather than the Venice of the Cotswolds, displaying the warts of speculative building and willow pattern bridges, and similarly Andoversford was offensive to him. Today when most modern houses are built of reconstituted stone, cast from a mixture of crushed stone and cement, the colouring may still correspond to the particular area of the Cotswolds, grey in the south, cream in the middle, honey in the north and russet in the east, but Andoversford continues with brick. Yet there are some brick structures such as the mill chimney at Lower Slaughter which contribute significantly to the scenic quality of the Cotswolds.

Old farm buildings also express the Cotswold style. This is particularly true of the great barns, tithe barns in the case of Stanway, Syde, Bourton-on-the-Hill and his favourite Great Coxwell, but also of those grouped at Hampnett, Beverstone, Newington Bagpath, Southrop, Ablington and Winson. Dovecotes too show the same style, more so with square than round ones, as at Naunton and Lower Slaughter.

The grouping of buildings receives special emphasis. Barns and houses at Siddington, castle, barns and farms at Beverstone, church, gatehouse and barn at Stanway, church, manor and cottages at Chavenage, mill and cottages at Bibury [fig. 90], farms and cottages like a flock of grey sheep at Througham, and many other combinations, illustrate this

90. HARMONY IN BUILDINGS AT BIBURY MILL

major theme, that a common material and craftsmen who knew the capability of the stone created a harmony and unity of buildings even though their dates span so many centuries. The buildings belong to the Cotswolds and their grouping underlines the fact.

The glory of the Cotswolds for Massingham was in its churches. He mentions fifty-five of them. He was not so much attracted to the hard, chilling splendour of the great showpiece wool churches of Chipping Campden, Fairford and Cirencester, which seemed to him more like a handsome bribe to heaven, and of which only Northleach had nobility, warmth and vitality but to the smaller details of the humbler buildings where so many examples of stone embroidery are to be found. The corbel heads at Kempsford and Aldsworth, a 'veritable aerial band' at Elkstone [fig. 91], the beakheads at Windrush and Siddington, the tympana at Quenington, Eastleach, Lower Swell and Elkstone, the gargoyles at Bourton-on-the-Hill, the tombs inside Sapperton church where he contrasts the reticent sixteenth-century memorials to the Pooles with the flamboyant eighteenth-century monument to Sir Robert Atkyns, commenting that these later squires went to heaven in style, and the finely carved tombs in Painswick churchyard, are some of the examples.

He also picks out features of the Oolite churches in the rather nondescript Vale villages, the ball flower decoration at Badgeworth, repeated at Bishops Cleeve with its splendid door frame of interlaced dragon tails, and Saxon Deerhurst with its decorated font.

Then there are the medieval crosses at Ashton Keynes, Ampney Crucis, Duntisbourne Rous and Condicote and the Norman chancel arches. Whether Saxon or Norman, Early English or Decorative, the carveable properties of the stone are exploited with consummate skill.

There is an apparent diversity in the sites of villages. Massingham follows the Churn valley and describes the sites of Elkstone on the crest, North Cerney on a valley side slope, Rendcomb on a headland, Cowley at a corner and Bagendon on a terrace. If however we regard water as the single most important site factor, we find that they are all close to springs with their regular supply of clean water and these are all located at the geological boundary between Oolite and clay. The assymetrical distribution of villages along the valley masks this common feature of spring location.

Four villages are given more attention than others, Upper and Lower Swell on the Dikler and Upper and Lower Slaughter on the Eye. These villages clearly illustrate the Cotswold balance between likeness and diversity. Their similarity is in their small size, their river location, their churches of Norman foundation on slightly higher ground and their signs of continuous occupation over several millenia. Massingham excels in his discussion of their diversity and typically identifies the features that unconsciously make Lower Slaughter, despite its manicured appearance, so attractive. He notices the bend in the line of the village as the road crosses from one side of the river to the other, the way that the houses are set at different distances from the river and at varied angles [fig. 92], and the siting of the old farms at right angles to the road up side alleys.

Similarly, selected streets of the market towns show the same variety of buildings but overall unity of expression. The best is the curving street in Chipping Campden from the parish church, past the ten gabled almshouses, William Grevel's house, the market hall and on to the smaller properties to the south-west, where five centuries of building are drawn together in 'stately consistency'. Another is the High Street in Tetbury.

As with our other Cotswold travel books there are personal reactions to these towns. Painswick for Massingham is trim, prim and precise, solemn, plump and matronly, but inwardly decaying. This is a comment on its Georgian prosperity and the later effects of northern industrialisation on the local cloth mills. And Broadway is an 'unpleasantness to be avoided', as the first town to exploit its Cotswold charm for commercial gain.

Massingham's interest in prehistory drew him to Belas Knap, where before its restoration, the earliest examples of drystone walling were to be seen in the ogee shaped forecourt, and to Hetty Pegler's Tump, one of the finest examples of long barrows. He thought that

91. CORBEL TABLE AT ELKSTONE. 'AN AERIAL BAND'

92. LOWER SLAUGHTER, HOUSES FACING IN DIFFERENT DIRECTIONS

the siting of long barrows was on high points with distinct views and that the Neolithic people were attracted to the Cotswolds by the availability of stone for their megalithic structures. He noted the concentration of long barrows around Lower Swell, the strangely unexcavated barrow in Lodge Park and the standing stones around Minchinhampton.

Having recently thought and written about the chalk landscapes, almost inevitably he makes comparisons between the Cotswolds and the downland regions of England, where the other soft limestone is found. Several interesting observations are also made on their contrasts. The first is with continuity of settlement. Both areas were populated in Neolithic times, when the Cotswold long barrows were constructed, and in Bronze and Iron Ages, when the escarpments were 'zoned by Celtic citadels'. But then settlement continued on the Cotswolds with Roman villa estates and then Saxon communities and so on to the present day, while the higher parts of the Downs were left largely unpopulated.

Another contrast is in their flora, where again the Cotswolds are more homely and Massingham notes how many Cotswold flowers are suitable for the cottage garden. Lily of the valley, columbine, pasque flower, fritillary and the hellebores are examples. He wrote before that sad phase of woodland management had occurred, when large-scale clearances of old woodland took place and replanting was often of quicker growing conifers, and so the lily of the valley that had flourished beneath the old oaks of Guiting Wood was nearly lost and woods are now less likely to 'change their suits with the seasons'.

Of other changes he was well aware. The displacement by machines of the traditional rural crafts of blacksmith, wheelwright, thatcher, hurdle- and basket-maker was regretted. Few stone masons were left. He mentions Hinchwick and Daglingworth as places where they could still be found. Early industry in the area produced things of beauty, financing churches, mills and houses; modern industry left scars, mutilation and desolation, as in the Stroud valleys. Nor did he favour the enclosure movement which brought poverty to many and, he says, the end of traditional building. He is unfair here, in that many new barns and farmhouses in the vernacular came with enclosure, and most of the drystone walls date from this time.

The selection of photographs chosen to illustrate the book are of great interest, in that they are pre-war timepieces. When taken of familiar scenes, for example Arlington Row, Owlpen or Naunton dovecote, they are not taken from the more conventional viewpoints. There are few if any cars, no double yellow lines, ploughing is by horse power, and hay and corn stacks are thatched. The streets and lanes are deserted but the fabric of the buildings has hardly altered. That timeless quality that Massingham so enjoyed is well illustrated.

His tour of the Cotswolds followed the river valleys, those of the Coln, Churn, Windrush, Leach and their tributaries. This is now regarded to be the best way to imbibe the atmosphere of the Cotswolds. But like Algernon Gissing he is taken into the heart of the Cotswolds by Buckle Street, running from Weston-sub-Edge over the widest stretch to Bourton-on-the-Water, thus revealing the wolds and giving Massingham his open spaces and sheep walks, fields of barley and sainfoin, coverts and copses, and glimpses into the valleys.

Sometimes he generalises from too small a sample, as with his reference to the pelican decoration at Saintbury. But the chief value of the book for those who know the area lies in his reflective thought about the scene he is describing. The destruction that must have taken place for the layout of Cirencester Park to feed the elegant whims of Earl Bathurst, the decorative exhuberance of the stone masons as they came to the edge of the Oolite outcrop, the way Cirencester streets combine Roman inflexibility with medieval twistiness and express opposed conceptions of life, and the way in which Chedworth Roman villa in its siting and mosaics shows how that most intractable mentality of Rome has been naturalised, are examples of this reflection. His landscape is an inward landscape half romantic, half scientific.

Some of his descriptions are memorable—meadow cranesbill compared to a tailor's sample of the sky, broomrape like a pallid caterpillar's body, wood anemones congregating like nebulæ—as perhaps one might expect from a professional journalist, educated at Westminster School and, like Gilpin, Queen's College, Oxford.

His obituary refers to him as a master anatomist of the English landscape, of its geological bones, its texture of living vegetation, its vesture and embroidery of human artifice and skill, and notes that what some critics mistook for an occasional affectation turned out on closer and more profound study to be an expression of spiritual struggle. This comment rings true for *Cotswold Country*.

Places to visit: Painswick's New Street, Elkstone for its church, Naunton for its setting, Lower Slaughter for its layout.